HAVE THE PROMISES FAILED?

SOCIETY
OF BIBLICAL
LITERATURE

DISSERTATION SERIES

William Baird, New Testament Editor
J. J. M. Roberts, Old Testament Editor

Gwendolyn B. Sayler

HAVE THE PROMISES FAILED?
A Literary Analysis of 2 Baruch

Scholars Press
Chico, California

HAVE THE PROMISES FAILED?

A Literary Analysis of 2 Baruch

Gwendolyn B. Sayler

BS
1775.2
.S28
1984

Ph.D., 1982
University of Iowa

Advisor:
George W. E. Nickelsburg

©1984
Society of Biblical Literature

Library of Congress Cataloging in Publication Data

Sayler, Gwendolyn B.
   Have the promises failed?

   (Dissertation series / Society of Biblical Literature ; no.
72)
   Bibliography: p.
   1. Bible. O.T. Apocrypha. Baruch, 2nd—Criticism,
interpretation, etc. I. Title. II. Series: Dissertation series
(Society of Biblical Literature) ; no. 72.
BS1775.2.S28 1984   229'.913   83-16336
ISBN 0-89130-651-X

Printed in the United States of America

Contents

Preface

The abbreviations used throughout this dissertation conform to the style suggested in the *Journal of Biblical Literature* 95 (1976) 331-46. Because the title "2 Baruch" occurs so frequently throughout the dissertation, I have not italicized it.

My first thanks are to the members of my committee in the University of Iowa School of Religion: Drs. George Nickelsburg, Helen Goldstein, Jonathan Goldstein, J. Kenneth Kuntz, and James McCue. Dr. Nickelsburg, my advisor, first introduced me to 2 Baruch and guided me through my entire program at Iowa. I appreciate his willingness to share his knowledge and his insistence that I be satisfied with nothing less than my best effort. Dr. Nickelsburg and Dr. Helen Goldstein read and analyzed each of the many drafts of this dissertation. They both made numerous suggestions, many of which have been incorporated in the dissertation.

I also want to thank the entire School of Religion faculty at Iowa for five years of mental stimulation and growth. Because of them and the graduate students studying under them, the University was an exciting place to pursue the study of religion. Finally, thanks are due to my faithful typist, Mary Lou Doyle. In addition to typing the dissertation, she also shared a wealth of helpful advice along the way.

The dissertation is dedicated to my family in North Dakota—Bette, Quentin, Tom, Valerie, Michael, and John Sayler.

I

Introduction

2 Baruch, or the Syriac Apocalypse of Baruch, is a pseudepigraphic Jewish document which is set on the eve of the destruction of Jerusalem in 587 B.C.E. Baruch, identified in the Scriptures as the scribe of Jeremiah, is the protagonist. He receives prophetic revelations from God and converses with God about the implications of the destruction for His power and justice. He also shares with his community the revelations he has received. His community, in turn, perceives that Baruch is the last leader remaining to them. The people listen to his speeches, and converse with him about the implications of his departure from them.

Generally, 2 Baruch is the title used to designate the whole of Chapters 1-87, which includes the *Apocalypse of Baruch* (chaps. 1-77) and the *Epistle of Baruch* (chaps. 78-87).[1] Here I shall use the title "2 Baruch" to refer to Chapters 1-77 only. The hypothesis that the Epistle was not a part of the original document will be defended below in Chapter III.

MANUSCRIPTS, EDITIONS, AND TRANSLATIONS

2 Baruch has been preserved in a limited number of manuscripts. The sole extant manuscript of the entire document, including the Epistle of Baruch, is a Syriac text of the sixth century C.E., MS B.21, in the Ambrosian Library at Milan.[2] An Arabic manuscript of Chapters 3-77 has been discovered in the Library of the Monastery of St. Catherine on Mt.

---

[1]For this usage, see, e.g., R. H.Charles, *Apocrypha and Pseudepigrapha of the Old Testament* (Oxford: Clarendon, 1913) 2. 470-526; P.-M. Bogaert, *Apocalypse de Baruch* (SC 144-45; Paris: Le Cerf, 1969).

[2]Manuscript B.21 Inf, fols 257a-265b. The manuscript was discovered by A. M. Ceriani in the nineteenth century. For a discussion, see Bogaert, *Apocalypse*, 1. 24-38.

Sinai.[3] It is scheduled for publication in the fall of 1982.[4] Fragments of
a few chapters of the book have been preserved in Greek in the Oxy-
rhynchus Papyrus fragment no. 403.[5] Moreover, some portions of
2 Baruch are also included in Jacobite lectionaries.[6]

The first edition of the Syriac manuscript was published by A. M.
Ceriani in 1871.[7] M. Kmosko produced another edition in 1907.[8] The text
of Chapters 1-77 of MS B.21 was most recently edited by S. Dedering in
1973.[9] I have used this edition as the textual basis of the dissertation.

R. H. Charles published an annotated English translation of
2 Baruch in 1896. The translation is prefaced by a brief introduction to
the book.[10] In 1913, he published a slightly revised edition of his translation in the *APOT*.[11] P.-M. Bogaert published a French translation of the
book with a lengthy introduction and a commentary in 1969.[12] The

---

[3]A. S. Atiya, *A Hand-list of the Arabic Manuscripts and Scrolls
Microfilmed at the Library of the Monastery of St. Catherine, Mt. Sinai*
(Baltimore, 1955) 24. The significance of the manuscript is discussed by
P. Sj. Van Koningsveld, "An Arabic Manuscript of the Apocalypse of
Baruch," *JSJ* 6 (1975) 205-7. Koningsveld doubts that the Arabic text is
a direct translation of the manuscript discovered by Ceriani. The primary
reason for his caution is that the Arabic manuscript clearly separates the
Apocalypse of Baruch from the *Epistle of Baruch*, while the Ceriani manuscript makes no clear distinction between the two documents. The first
folio of the text, containing Chapters 1-2 of 2 Baruch, is missing.
    [4]The text will be published by E. J. Brill in Leiden. See the *SBL
Pseudepigrapha Newsletter*, No. 18, May 1982.
    [5]Chapters 12; 13:1-2, 11-12; and 14:1-3. See R. H. Charles, *APOT*,
2.487-90; B. P. Grenfell and A. S. Hunt, *The Oxyrhynchos Papyri* (London,
1903) 3.3-7 and pl.1 (recto). The Greek fragment was re-edited by A.-M.
Denis, *Fragmenta pseudepigraphorum quae supersunt graeca* (PVTG 3;
Leiden; E. J. Brill, 1970) 118-20.
    [6]See Bogaert, *Apocalypse*, 1.38-40.
    [7]A. M. Ceriani, ed., "Apocalypsis Syriace Baruch," *Monumenta Sacra
et Profana* (Mediolani: Bibliotheca Ambrosiana, 1871) 5. 113-80.
    [8]M. Kmosko, *Liber Apocalypseos Baruch filii Neriae . . . Epistola
Baruch filii Neriae* (Patrologia Syriaca, 1.2; Paris: Firmin-Didot et Socii,
1907) 1056-1205. Kmosko included a Latin translation of the text.
    [9]S. Dedering, ed., "The Apocalypse of Baruch," *The Old Testament
in Syriac* 4.3 (Leiden: E. J. Brill, 1973).
    [10]R. H. Charles, *The Apocalypse of Baruch* (London: Black, 1896;
repr. London: SPCK, 1917; repr. 1929).
    [11]Charles, *APOT*, 2.470-526.
    [12]Bogaert, *Apocalypse*.

document has been translated into German by A. F. J. Klijn (1976), who also includes a brief introduction.[13] Except where noted, my quotations are taken from Charles' 1913 translation, with some modifications in style.

THE ORIGINAL LANGUAGE

The original language of 2 Baruch is unknown. R. H. Charles argues that the Syriac text is a translation of a Greek translation of a Hebrew text.[14] After examining the issue thoroughly, P.-M. Bogaert concludes that the Syriac text is a translation from a Greek document. Although he does not exclude the possibility, Bogaert doubts that the Greek document was dependent on a Hebrew original.[15]

THE DATE OF COMPOSITION

The exact date of composition of 2 Baruch is unknown. Although a few scholars have dated it ca. 63 B.C.E., there is a broad consensus that it was composed sometime between 70 and 132 C.E. The various hypotheses regarding the date of composition will be examined below in Chapter IV.[16]

HISTORY OF RESEARCH

2 Baruch has not been the object of intense scholarly scrutiny. The three major treatments of the book are those of R. H. Charles, P.-M. Bogaert, and W. Harnisch. In addition, A. C. B. Kolenkow has examined the two visions of the book, and A. Thompson has included a partial analysis of 2 Baruch in his study of the theodicy of 4 Ezra.[17]

---

[13]A. F. J. Klijn, "Die syrische Baruch-Apokalypse," *Jüdische Schriften aus hellenistisch-römischer Zeit* 5.2 (Gütersloh: Gerd Mohn, 1976).
[14]Charles, *APOT*, 2. 471-74. A modern scholar who defends the theory of a Hebrew original is F. Zimmerman, "Textual Observations on the Apocalypse of Baruch," *JTS* 40 (1939) 151-56.
[15]Bogaert, *Apocalypse*, 1.380.
[16]See below, pp. 103-10.
[17]R. H. Charles, *Apocalypse*; Idem, *APOT*, 2. 470-526; P.-M. Bogaert, *Apocalypse*; W. Harnisch, *Verhängnis und Verheissung der Geschichte: Untersuchungen zum Zeit- und Geschichtsverständnis im*

R. H. Charles

In addition to translating 2 Baruch into English, R. H. Charles attempts to determine its structure and to summarize its content.[18] His conclusions about the book are evident in his introductory comments:

> The Apocalypse of Baruch . . . is a composite work written in the latter half of the first century of the Christian era. Its authors were orthodox Jews, and it is a good representative of the Judaism against which the Pauline dialectic was addressed. . . . This Apocalypse is, as has already been stated, composite. The editor has made use of a number of independent writings, belonging to various dates between 50-90 A.D. They are thus contemporaneous with the chief New Testament writings, and furnish records of the Jewish doctrines and beliefs of that period, . . . with which its leaders sought to uphold its declining faith and confront the attack of a growing and aggressive Christianity. Written by Pharisaic Jews as an apology for Judaism, and in part, an implicit polemic against Christianity, it nevertheless gained a large circulation.[19]

Charles' conclusions about the composite structure of 2 Baruch must be understood in the context of the multiple source methodology which was popular at the turn of the twentieth century. The basic axiom of this methodology was that a document must be interally consistent; the presence of differing viewpoints in any given work was attributed to the use of multiple sources by the author or redactor.[20] Using this methodology,

---

4 Buch Esra und in der syr. Baruchapokalypse (FRLANT 97; Göttingen: Vandenhoeck und Ruprecht, 1969); A. C. B. Kolenkow, *An Introduction to Baruch 53, 56-74: Structure and Substance* (Harvard Ph.D., 1971); A. Thompson, *Responsibility for Evil in the Theodicy of 4 Ezra* (SBLDS 29; Missoula: Scholars Press, 1977).

Bogaert (*Apocalypse*, 2. 165-203) has compiled an extensive bibliography of 2 Baruch research. For bibliographical information, see also J. Charlesworth, *The Pseudepigrapha and Modern Research with a Supplement* (SCS 7; Chico: Scholars Press, 1981) 83-86, 275.

[18]Charles, *APOT*, 2. 470-80.

[19]Ibid., 470.

[20]This type of methodology is described in relation to 4 Ezra research by M. Stone, *Features of the Eschatology in 4 Ezra* (Harvard Ph.D., 1965) 11-21.

Charles argues that 2 Baruch is dependent on two different types of documents—one optimistic about the future of Israel on earth and the other pessimistic in this regard. He then subdivides the two types of documents into six major sources and several fragments of yet other sources. Charles concludes his examination of the structure of 2 Baruch by stating:

> The solution here offered seems extremely complex, but since the problem is almost incredibly complex, the solution cannot be a simple or obvious one. Further investigation will no doubt modify some of the above conclusions, but I know of no study since my edition in 1896 that gives adequate grounds for any serious departure from the above analysis.[21]

Charles' conclusions about the content of 2 Baruch are based on a topical examination of each of the sources which he has identified by means of his method. In great part because of his assumption that 2 Baruch describes "the Pharisaic perspective," Charles' choice of topics is governed by his conviction that "(2 Baruch) . . . is of great value to the New Testament student, as it furnishes him with the historical setting and background of many of the New Testament problems."[22] The topics which he considers include: original sin and free-will, the law, works and justification, the Messiah and the Messianic kingdom, and the resurrection.[23]

Subsequent developments in biblical research require that we modify Charles' conclusions about the structure of 2 Baruch. We now know that Jewish authors of the Greco-Roman period frequently integrated a variety of sources and traditions into an individual document, with no attempt to harmonize different or even conflicting viewpoints. The use of several of these sources and traditions by a creative author does not negate the literary unity of his work.[24] Thus, any methodological

---

[21]Charles, *APOT*, 2. 476.

[22]Ibid., 477.

[23]Ibid., 477-79.

[24]See Stone, *Features*, 21-29. For a discussion of the historical development of biblical criticism in this direction, see H. Frei, *Eclipse of Biblical Narrative* (New Haven: Yale University Press, 1974). For a discussion of the present state of biblical literary criticism, see A. N. Wilder, *Early Christian Rhetoric* (Cambridge: Harvard University Press, 1971) xxii; and R. Polzin, *Moses and the Deuteronomist* (New York: Seabury, 1980) xi.

approach to the literary structure of an individual document should include the question: "how do all the various parts work together to develop the whole?". Because of the question Charles addresses to the text ("how can we break the redacted whole into its original sources?"), his conclusions about the literary structure of 2 Baruch fail to do justice to the document as a literary unity.

Subsequent developments in research on Jewish thought in the first century C.E. require that we also modify Charles' conclusions about the type of Judaism reflected by the content of 2 Baruch. We now know that Jewish thought was in a great deal of flux at this time. There simply was no such entity as "the orthodox, Pharisaic Judaism of this period."[25] Thus, Charles inaccurately assumes that the topics he discovers in 2 Baruch represent the orthodox Pharisaic perspective on the types of problems discussed in the New Testament. This assumption prevents him from approaching 2 Baruch as a document in its own right, apart from any relationship to "Pharisaism" or to the New Testament.

P.-M. Bogaert

P.-M. Bogaert acknowledges the inadequacy of R. H. Charles' approach to 2 Baruch, and defends the unity of composition of the document. Using the seven episode structure of 4 Ezra as a model, Bogaert devises criteria which enable him to argue that 2 Baruch follows a similar seven-episode pattern.[26] By defending the unity of composition of the book, Bogaert has made a valuable contribution to 2 Baruch research. However, while he has argued convincingly that the parts of 2 Baruch do comprise a literary whole, he has not shown how they are related to each other and are integrated into a literary unity.

Bogaert, like Charles before him, employs a topical approach to the content of 2 Baruch. He describes the goal of his chapter on the theological content of 2 Baruch as follows:

---

[25]For an excellent example of the diversity of Jewish thought in this time period, see J. Neusner, *Judaism: The Evidence of the Mishnah* (Chicago: University of Chicago Press, 1981) 5-14, 25-44.

[26]Bogaert, *Apocalypse*, 1. 56-81. Bogaert divides the episodes as follows: 1:1-12:4; 12:5-20:6; 21-34; 35:1-47:1; 47:2-52:7; 53:1-77:17; 77:18-87:1.   His criteria include: place changes, weeks of fasting, encounters of Baruch with his people, and the writing of the *Epistle of Baruch*.

Le but de ce chapitre [est] . . . de décrire la théologie profes-
sée et enseignée par l'auteur de l'*Apocalypse de Baruch* en la
comparant avec de l'Apocalypse d'Esdras—si proche par tant
d'aspects—et avec celles des docteurs tannaïtes.[27]

His methodology consists of arranging the theological content of 2 Baruch
according to topics (the great themes of suffering and of the Torah,
names for God, anthropology, proselytism and universalism, eschatology,
angelology) and comparing quotes from 2 Baruch with similar material in
4 Ezra and rabbinic writings.[28] This topical approach does enable Bogaert
to isolate some of the main themes of 2 Baruch. In this regard, he once
again has made a valuable contribution to 2 Baruch research. However,
by atomizing the text into topics, he has left unanswered the question of
the relationship of the individual themes to each other and to the whole
composition. The criticism of his argument about the structure of
2 Baruch applies also to his analysis of the book's content.

W. Harnisch

W. Harnisch has examined in depth the relationship between time
and history in 2 Baruch and 4 Ezra.[29] By explicating the eschatological
dimensions of the vindication of God's justice and power, he has made an
important contribution to one aspect of 2 Baruch research. However,
because he has treated this theme in isolation from its context in the
book, Harnisch has not dealt with the question of how the theme functions
and is developed within the literary structure of 2 Baruch.

A. C. B. Kolenkow

A. C. B. Kolenkow isolates the two visions of 2 Baruch (chaps. 36-40,
53-74) and argues that this material is dependent on 4 Ezra 4, 11-13, and
is intended as a corrective to Ezra's view of the end-times.[30] She does
not raise the question of how the visionary material fits into the structure
of either book.

27Ibid., 1. 383.
28Ibid., 1. 381-444.
29Harnisch, *Verhängnis*.
30Kolenkow, *Introduction*, 1-31.

A. Thompson

The research of A. Thompson represents yet another methodological approach to 2 Baruch. Thompson suggests that a joint analysis of certain parts of 2 Baruch and 4 Ezra can illumine the meaning of both books.[31] Because his major interest is 4 Ezra, it is not surprising that the agenda of 4 Ezra provides the basis for the questions he addresses to 2 Baruch. As a result of the joint analysis of the two books, Thompson asserts that "the dominant trend of the book (2 Baruch) is that man is quite capable of obeying God's commands and therefore is able to gain future bliss by merit."[32] Thompson's research is significant as an example of the interpretation of 2 Baruch in the light of 4 Ezra. The question of whether 2 Baruch has its own, unique agenda is simply not addressed.

PROSPECTUS OF THE DISSERTATION

In this dissertation, I will examine 2 Baruch as a literary whole, seeking to draw out of its parts the message of the document. I will discuss the book as a piece of theological literature which is making its own specific response to the events of 70 C.E. These considerations notwithstanding, the catalyst for my approach to 2 Baruch has been an article on 4 Ezra by E. Breech.[33] He summarizes his approach to 4 Ezra as follows:

> This paper [about the form and function of 4 Ezra] has been written with the conviction that the structure and meaning of 4 Ezra are mutually determinative. I would suggest that the formal principle which structures 4 Ezra as a literary composition is what may be called the pattern of consolation. The form of the work is constituted by the narrative of Ezra's movement from distress to consolation, from distress occasioned by the destruction of Jerusalem, to consolation by the Most High himself who reveals to the prophet, in dream visions, his end-time plans.[34]

---

[31] Thompson, *Responsibility*, 121-55, 294-353.
[32] Ibid., 133.
[33] Earl Breech, "These Fragments I Have Shored against My Ruins: The Form and Function of 4 Ezra," *JBL* 92 (1973) 267-74.
[34] Ibid., 269.

In what follows, I will argue that the key to the structure of 2 Baruch is the pattern identified by Breech in relation to 4 Ezra. The author of 2 Baruch responds to the events of 70 C.E. by composing a story—a story in which Baruch and then his community move from grief to consolation. The story is carried by sections of narrative prose, which are supplemented by units of other literary genres (laments, a discourse, prayers, conversation, and visions). By means of this story, the author develops the issues with which he is concerned. He does this by clustering the various units and arranging them into seven major blocks of material, in which he raises and then resolves the issues of the book. The result is a coherent and artistic document, which moves smoothly from its beginning to its conclusion.

Chapter II of the dissertation will deal with the structure of 2 Baruch. I will trace the unfolding of the story through the author's arrangement of the various literary units into larger blocks of material. The analysis will reveal that two primary issues are raised and resolved throughout the course of the story: the vindication of God as just and powerful in the wake of the destruction; and the survival of the faithful Jewish community in the aftermath of the destruction.

Chapter III will utilize the analysis of the structure of 2 Baruch in order to examine its content more thoroughly. I will plot the development of each of the primary issues throughout the blocks of material. In so doing, I will explicate on the basis of terminology, concepts, and structure how the blocks are related to each other within the literary whole.

Chapter IV will discuss what can be learned from 2 Baruch about the historical circumstances to which the author is responding. I will deal with hypotheses about the date of composition and will attempt to draw out of the text clues to the author's perception of his real world.

Chapter V will compare the response of 2 Baruch to the destruction with the responses of four related documents—Pseudo-Philo, 4 Ezra, the *Apocalypse of Abraham*, the *Paraleipomena of Jeremiah*, and the Gospel of Matthew. The comparison will illustrate the similarities and differences in these responses to the events with which they are concerned.

Chapter VI will summarize and synthesize the findings of the dissertation. I will also raise several questions which need to be treated in future research on 2 Baruch.

II

The Literary Structure
of 2 Baruch

INTRODUCTION

The length and complexity of 2 Baruch complicate the task of determining its literary structure. P.-M. Bogaert's division of the book into seven episodes is thus far the most cogent effort to defend its unity of composition and to find a coherent structure in the text.[1] Much of Bogaert's research on 2 Baruch contributes to a clearer understanding of the document. However, while he has argued convincingly that the individual parts of 2 Baruch do comprise a whole, Bogaert has not shown how those parts are related to each other and are integrated into a literary unity. It is precisely this literary unity which I will attempt to spell out in this chapter.

A superficial reading of 2 Baruch reveals that it is comprised of several kinds of literary units which can be designated by formal literary criteria. Throughout the book, the reader encounters sections of narrative prose (e.g., 1:1; 77:18-26). A variety of speech units also are scattered throughout the book. For example, there are prayers (e.g., 21:4-25; chap. 38), laments (10:6-11:7; chap. 35), a discourse (12:1-4), and conversations (e.g., 1:2-5:4; chaps. 13-20). In addition, the book contains two visions (chaps. 36-37; 53:1b-11).

In what follows, I will argue that the author of 2 Baruch has organized his work by clustering and arranging the individual literary units so that they constitute sub-units of larger blocks of material. Each of these blocks is a unified literary whole and has its own function within the total structure of the document. Throughout the dissertation, I will use the

---

[1] P.-M. Bogaert, *Apocalypse de Baruch* (SC 144-45; Paris: Le Cerf, 1969) 1. 58-67.

phrase "block(s) of material" as a technical term to describe the literary whole(s) created by the clusters of individual literary sub-units.[2]

My method of determining the extent of each block of material is based on two criteria: disparity and inner coherence. The criterion of disparity is used to ascertain where one block of material ends and another begins. By bringing to the foreground the factors which indicate disjunction, I will attempt to determine the boundaries of each block of material. These boundaries are not always clear-cut; sometimes there is overlap between two blocks (e.g., Blocks 1 and 2—5:5-6:1ff.) and in one case the normal pattern of clusters is truncated (Block 6—chaps. 53-76, where the normal narrative introductory material is lacking). The criterion of inner coherence is used to ascertain the unity of a block on the basis of subject matter. Essential to this criterion is common subject matter or the development of a common theme throughout the related literary sub-units (e.g., the narrative, lament, discourse, and conversation of chaps. 6-20). As the analysis progresses, it will become apparent that there is a definite symmetry between the structures of various blocks of material (Blocks 2 and 4, 3 and 5, 1 and 7). This symmetry will support the designation of the individual literary wholes as blocks of material, and will illustrate how the blocks are related to each other in terms of content.

After I have described the boundaries of a block of material and have demonstrated its inner coherence, I will briefly discuss its function within the book. It will become apparent that the individual blocks of material relate to one another as parts of an unfolding, coherent, artistic composition.

The analysis of the structure of 2 Baruch will reveal that the author has clustered and arranged the individual literary sub-units into blocks of material in order to tell a story—a story in which Baruch and then his community move from grief to consolation. By tracing the

---

[2]My awareness of the importance of the clustering and arranging of the literary sub-units is indebted to the methodological approach of N. Peterson, "The Composition of Mark 4:1-8:26," *HTR* 73 (1980) 184-217. Peterson shows how the literary whole of the Markan text is based on the use of minimal literary units as building blocks of the larger unity. In so doing, he is able to utilize the consensus of scholarship about the general boundaries of the literary whole with which he is dealing. In contrast, I must use my own formal criteria to spell out the boundaries of each of the literary wholes in 2 Baruch.

development of the story through the blocks of material, I will identify the issues with which the author is concerned.

Prior to the actual analysis of the text, it is helpful to identify precisely what I mean by "individual literary sub-units." To a large extent, these sub-units conform to form-critical categories. In some instances, my terminology for the sub-units is less technical.

The first type of literary sub-unit is narrative prose. The story is carried by sections of this prose. Frequently, the narrative sections function as brief introductions (e.g., 10:5; 13:1) or conclusions (e.g., 21:26; 53:12) to other sub-units. One narrative section constitutes a fairly lengthy description of the fall of Jerusalem (6:1-10:4).

The second type of literary sub-unit is comprised of sections of speech. These include the following:

Laments by Baruch—10:6-11:7; chap. 35

A discourse by Baruch—12:1-4

Prayers by Baruch—21:4-25; chap. 38; 48:2-24; chap. 54

Conversations between God and Baruch—1:2-5:4; chaps. 13-20; chaps. 22-30; chaps. 39-43; 48:26-52:7

A conversation between Ramiel and Baruch—55:4-76:4

Speeches by Baruch—31:3-32:7; 44:2-45:2; 77:2-10

Conversations between Baruch and his community—32:8-34:1; chap. 46; 77:11-17

The third type of literary sub-unit is visions. There are two visions (chaps. 36-37; 53:1b-11), each of which is interpreted for Baruch in subsequent sub-units of conversation (chaps. 39-40; 56-74).

The blocks of material formed by the arrangement of the sub-units constitute the subdivisions of the following analysis. The boundaries of each block are as follows:

Block 1—Chapters 1-5

Block 2—Chapters 6-20

Block 3—Chapters 21-30

Block 4—Chapters 31-43

Block 5—Chapters 44-52

Block 6—Chapters 53-76

Block 7—Chapter 77

An outline of the structure of 2 Baruch is located in the Appendix. Throughout my analysis, I will key each literary sub-unit according to the outline.

ANALYSIS OF THE LITERARY STRUCTURE OF 2 BARUCH

Block 1—Chapters 1-5

Block 1 consists of a narrative introduction (1:1), a conversation between God and Baruch (1:2-5:4), and a narrative conclusion (5:5-7).

Narrative Introduction (1 A)

The narrative introduction (1:1) establishes the fictional setting of the story as the days prior to the fall of Jerusalem to Babylon in 587 B.C.E. An integral part of the narrative introduction is the formula ". . . the Word of God came . . . and said," which introduces the conversation. The use of the past tense in the introductory formula makes the conversation part of the story which began with the narrative introduction, which was also in the past tense. This literary device is used throughout the book to integrate the speech segments and the visions into the story.[3]

Conversation (1 B)

Conversation begins (1:2-4) as God tells Baruch that the city will be destroyed because of the people's sins. Baruch is to lead those who are like him outside the city so that their works and prayers can no longer protect it. The destruction will be temporary, as will be the dispersion of the people (1:4).

Baruch reacts to this revelation with a death-wish and a series of questions (3:4-9) which reduce to three: How will Israel survive? What will be the future of the world? Are God's words to Moses about Israel still efficacious?

God responds to these questions by reemphasizing the temporary nature of the destruction and the chastening of the people (4:1). His

---

[3]Because brief narrative introductory or concluding phrases occur so frequently throughout the book, they generally either have been omitted from the outline (Appendix), or have been included with the sections they introduce or conclude. My awareness of the importance of the story which is carried by these narrative sections is indebted to the discussion of the structure of 4 Ezra by E. Breech, "These Fragments I have Shored against My Ruins: The Form and Function of 4 Ezra," *JBL* 92 (1973) 267-74.

description of the heavenly Temple (4:2-6) alludes to the eschatological resolution of the present crisis.[4]

Before Baruch obeys God's exhortation to go and do as He had commanded him (4:7), he raises one more matter: his grief that the enemy will destroy God's city and then return home to boast before their idols (5:1). God assures him that the enemy will not overthrow the city (5:2-3).

Narrative Conclusion (1 C)

The narrative conclusion (5:5-7) recounts how Baruch leads the honorable men out of the city to the Kidron valley. He tells them what he has heard, and together they weep and fast until evening.

Conclusion

Several factors indicate that Chapters 1-5 constitute a major block of material. The first day of the story begins as God tells Baruch to lead those who are like him outside the city (chap. 2); it concludes as Baruch does so and shares with them the revelation he has received (5:5-7). A time reference ("we fasted until the evening," 5:7) indicates the termination of the day's activities and provides a break between them and the action to follow on the morrow.

The unified subject matter of Chapters 1-5 also identifies this text as one block of material. Baruch's questions and God's replies (3:1-5:4) deal with a single set of issues: the immediate implications of the impending destruction which God has just announced to Baruch (chap. 1). It is precisely this revelation which Baruch shares with the honorable men in the narrative conclusion to the day's activities (5:5-7).

The function of this block is introductory: it establishes the setting of the story, announces the action that is to follow, and identifies as a primary concern of the author the implications of the destruction for the future of Israel and the nations.

Block 2—Chapters 6-20

Block 2 consists of a narrative (6:1-10:4), a lament (10:6-11:7), a

---

[4]See below, pp. 66-67.

discourse (12:1-4), and a conversation between God and Baruch (chaps. 13-20).

Narrative (2 A)

The narrative at the end of Block 1 continues in the author's description of the second day of the story (6:1-8:2). Baruch departs from the honorable men in the Kidron valley and is lifted over the walls of Jerusalem.[5] There, he receives visual confirmation of God's earlier assurance that the enemy would not overthrow the city (1B—5:1-3). After the enemy has seized the city, Baruch and Jeremiah mourn and fast for a week. Then Baruch instructs Jeremiah to join the exiles in Babylon, while he remains in the Temple ruins to receive revelations about the last days (8:3-10:4).

Lament (2 B)

As he sits in the Temple ruins, Baruch utters a lengthy lament (10:6-11:7). It is bracketed by death-wishes (10:6; 11:6-7), and contains exhortations that all life cease functioning because of the desolation of Mother Zion. Near the end of the lament, Baruch interrupts his exhortations to tell Babylon that Jewish grief is infinite because she prospers while Zion is desolate (11:1-2). This interjection anticipates his subsequent discourse.

Discourse (2 C)

The destiny of Babylon is the subject of this discourse (12:1-4). Baruch warns Babylon that her prosperity will not endure for all time; in its time, divine anger, now restrained by long-suffering, will awake against her. After the discourse, Baruch fasts seven days (12:5) before God once again converses with him.

---

[5]The terms "Jerusalem," "Zion," "the city," and "the Temple" will be treated as synonymous and therefore interchangeable, unless otherwise indicated. The practice of using the terms interchangeably was common in this time period. For a summary of the various ways in which this terminology was used, see G. Fohrer and E. Lohse, "Siōn," TDNT 7 (1971) 300-20.

Conversation (2 D)

God opens the conversation (chaps. 13-20) by explaining His method of chastening the nations and Israel (chap. 13). He tells Baruch that the present prosperity of the enemy cities is only temporary. Retribution will fall on them at the consummation; then they will be completely punished for their continuous misuse of creation and their rejection of God's beneficence.[6] In contrast, the present chastisement of Israel is temporary and will lead to her pardon.

The reference to the prosperous cities (13:4) connects this revelation to Baruch's discourse (12:1-4) and to his address to Babylon within his lament (11:1-2). God elaborates what Baruch asserted in his discourse by setting the final retribution against Babylon within the context of His method of chastening the nations and Israel.[7]

God's explanation of His method of chastening the nations and Israel is unacceptable to Baruch for two reasons: (1) too few Gentiles will be left at the consummation to experience the promised retribution (14:1-3); and (2) the destruction of Zion, despite the righteousness of some of its inhabitants, only demonstrates the futility of righteousness (14:4-7). Baruch reiterates his frustration by concluding that God's ways are incomprehensible (14:8-19).

God defers Baruch's question about the delay in retribution against the nations until a later conversation (3 C—chaps. 22-30). In response to Baruch's second assertion, He defends the justness of His present dealings with Israel. The basis of God's defense is the eschatological destinies of the wicked and righteous within Israel (chap. 15). Each Jew is responsible

---

[6]Within this segment, the object of God's retribution is described first as the now prosperous cities (13:4) and then as the peoples and nations (13:11).

[7]Bogaert (*Apocalypse*, 1. 58-69) argues that Episode 2 begins at 13:1. There are two problems with this position. First, Bogaert does not observe that God's revelation to Baruch in 13:1ff. is connected to Baruch's discourse (12:1-4) and lament (10:6-11:7) by the reiteration of the prosperity motif. The revelation continues a line of thought rather than initiating a new unit. Secondly, Bogaert's division is based on the premise that Chapter 12 is part of Baruch's lament. Here Bogaert does not note that the death-wishes of Baruch (10:6; 11:6-7) form the logical borders of the lament. He then also does not see how Baruch's discourse (12:1-4), which he classes as part of the lament, moves beyond the words addressed to Babylon in the lament.

for his/her decision vis-à-vis God. Because violators of the Torah transgressed the covenant with conscious intent, they will suffer torment. This
world is a place of suffering for the righteous; however, the future world
will be a crown of great glory for them. God's defense does not satisfy Baruch. His complaint that time is
too short to acquire the measureless (chap. 16) introduces a new part of
the conversation. God uses the example of the life spans and legacies of
Adam and Moses to argue that the shortened life span resulting from
Adam's sin does not negate the individual's ability to choose his/her destiny (chap. 17). Baruch replies that few Jews have imitated Moses. On
the contrary, many Jews have chosen the darkness of Adam (chap. 18).[8]
God responds to this concern (19:1-3) by paraphrasing Deuteronomy 30:15-
20 as a reminder that the stipulations of the covenant still are in effect.

God encourages Baruch to anticipate the consummation, instead of
despairing over the present shameful treatment of the righteous (19:4-8).
After exhorting him to retain what he has learned, God brings the conver-
sation to a conclusion by giving him instructions and a promise (20:3-6).
He instructs Baruch to go and sanctify himself and then to return to Mt.
Zion.[9] He promises that then He will reveal Himself again and will tell
Baruch about the method of the times.

Conclusion

The text of Chapters 6-20 is identifiable as a block of material on
several grounds. The changes in time, location, and characters indicate
that a new section begins with 6:1ff. The exhortation, instructions, and
promise which conclude God's conversation with Baruch (20:3-6) form a
natural ending to the block. God's exhortation that Baruch retain what he
has learned functions as a summary of the preceding revelation, while the
promise that Baruch will receive information about the method of the
times anticipates subsequent revelation. The instructions separate the

---

[8]The text reads ". . . he that lighted took from the lamp, and few
are those who imitated him. But many of those he lit took from the darkness of Adam, and did not rejoice in the light of the lamp" (chap. 18).

[9]The text reads "that place" (20:6). Throughout the book, Mt. Zion
is the scene of God's revelations to Baruch. The connection between "that
place" and Mt. Zion in this particular instance is indicated by the reference to Mt. Zion earlier in the conversation (13:1) and by the subsequent
comment that after his fast Baruch came to "the place where God had
spoken to him" (21:2).

two revelations; moreover, together with the promise they provide an outline of the next block. The changes in location and subject matter with which that section begins also distinguish it from the material which precedes it. The development of a common theme throughout the related literary sub-units also supports the designation of this section of text as a block of material. That theme is the relationship of God's justice to the present prosperity of Babylon and to the desolation of Zion. Baruch witnesses the destruction (6:1-8:2; cf. 1 A and B—chap. 1) and reacts to it through his lament (10:6-11:7) and discourse (12:1-4). The contrast between Zion's desolation and Babylon's prosperity, emphasized in the lament and implied in the discourse, provides the backdrop for God's comments in the subsequent conversation (chaps. 13-20). God explains how the present prosperity of Babylon and the present punishment of Israel are part of His method of administering justice by chastening the nations and Israel. The questions raised by Baruch in response to this explanation (14:1-7) are the foil used by God to defend the justness of His present dealings with Israel (chaps. 15-19). The basis of His defense is the eschatological destinies of the righteous and the wicked within Israel (chaps. 15:1-19:3). God's exhortation to Baruch to anticipate the consummation rather than despairing over that which prospers in the present (19:4-8) connects the conversation back to the lament and discourse which prompted it.

The function of Block 2 (chaps. 6-20) is twofold. It introduces the issue of the relationship between the destruction of Jerusalem and God's method of dispensing justice to the nations and to Israel. In so doing, it explicates the first part of God's earlier conversation with Baruch (1 B— 1:2-4:1). It also introduces the contrast between the righteous and the wicked within Israel.

The conversation between God and Baruch brings to a temporary conclusion the discussion of God's justice toward the nations and Israel. As promised by God (20:6), the subsequent discussion will deal with the unfolding of the method of the times.[10]

---

[10]Bogaert (*Apocalypse,* 1. 58-69) also suggests that Episode 2 concludes at 20:6. His criterion is the instructions to Baruch to fast for seven days. Bogaert's concentration solely on the fast obscures the crucial shift in perspective at this point. He also does not observe that the instructions and promise provide an outline for the structure of the next block of material. Thus, he does not see how the material in this unit moves the story forward.

Block 3—Chapters 21-30

Block 3 consists of a narrative introduction (21:1-3), a prayer (21:4-25), and a lengthy conversation between God and Baruch (chaps. 22-30).

Narrative Introduction (3 A)

The narrative continues as Baruch leaves the Temple area and goes alone to the Kidron valley. There he obeys the first instruction given to him (cf. 20:5) by sanctifying himself and fasting seven days (21:1-2). After the week has passed, he carries out the second instruction (cf. 20:6) by returning to Mt. Zion (21:3), which is the setting for his prayer.

Prayer (3 B)

Baruch's prayer (21:4-25) reveals his impatience with the delay in the manifestation of God's power caused by His long-suffering. The prayer begins with an acknowledgment of God's power over creation and of His knowledge of the consummation of the times (21:4-12). After asking how long the present world and time will continue (21:19), Baruch petitions God to show His power to the nations. Then they will know that His long-suffering is not weakness (21:20-21).

The reference to God's long-suffering indicates that Baruch here is pleading that God implement immediately the judgment which Baruch announced in his discourse (2 C—12:1-4). By expressing concern that God's failure to exercise His power will be misperceived as weakness, Baruch also returns to a theme in his initial conversation with God—the relationship of God's power to the enemy's triumph over His city (1 B—5:1-3). Here, as there, Baruch is concerned with all Israel in contrast to the nations.[11]

The prayer concludes as Baruch expresses his desire that God seal Sheol and let the treasuries of souls restore those persons preserved in them (21:22-24). A sense of urgency is evident in his final plea that God show His glory quickly and not delay what He has promised (21:25).

---

[11]We will see that Baruch defines "Israel" as the few Jews who are faithful to the Mosaic covenant. See below, Chapter III.

Conversation (3 C)

In the subsequent conversation (chaps. 22-30), Baruch's impatience over the delay in the manifestation of God's power is resolved by a glimpse of God's plan for mankind. As He indicated He would do (cf. 20:6), God again reveals Himself and speaks to Baruch. He uses Baruch's impatience as a foil to illustrate that consolation is possible only when a project is completed (chap. 22). Then He tells Baruch that the present time is only one segment in His plan for mankind, which extends throughout time (chap. 23). The consummation cannot come until the full number of souls, predetermined when Adam sinned, has been born (23:4-5). At that time, the resurrection sought by Baruch (cf. 21:22-25) will occur (24:1-2).

In response to Baruch's query regarding how much time is left (24:3-4), God describes in considerable detail the twelve parts of the last times, the Messianic era of peace and fecundity, and the resurrection (chaps. 25-30). He concludes the conversation by contrasting the joy of the risen righteous with the progressive wasting away of the wicked (30:2-5).

Conclusion

Several factors indicate that the end of this conversation brings to a conclusion a block of material. The activity outlined at the conclusion of the preceding block (". . . go and sanctify yourself . . . come to that place . . . I will reveal myself and speak . . ." 20:5-6) has been completed. Moreover, changes in location, characters, and issues will distinguish the material which follows from the section of the text we have just discussed.

The development of a common theme throughout the related literary sub-units also supports the designation of this section as one block. That theme is the time remaining until the consummation. After he has sanctified himself (21:1-3), Baruch prays that God show His power to the nations immediately (21:4-25). In the conversation which follows, God chides Baruch for this impatience and describes His plan for mankind, which extends throughout time. Baruch learns that the present time is only one segment in a vast scenario extending from the creation to the consummation. All the steps in God's plan must be completed prior to the consummation (chaps. 22-30).

The function of Block 3 (chaps. 21-30) is to introduce the problem of the perceived delay in the manifestation of God's power to the nations.

Baruch's impatience is countered by a description of God's plan for mankind.

Block 4—Chapters 31-43

Block 4 consists of a narrative introduction (31:1-2), Baruch's speech to the elders of his community (31:3-32:7), a conversation between Baruch and his people (32:8-34:1), a lament (chap. 35), a vision (chaps. 36-37), a prayer (chap. 38), and a conversation between God and Baruch (chaps. 39-43).

Narrative and Speech (4 A and B)

The narrative continues as Baruch goes to his people and tells them to assemble the elders in the Kidron valley (31:1-2).[12] They do so, and Baruch delivers a speech to them (31:3-32:7). His message is succinct and reflects the revelation he has just received. He warns the elders that the present disaster is a prelude to worse tribulations in the final times. Nevertheless, if the people prepare their hearts and sow in them the fruits of the Torah, the Torah will protect them on the day when God does shake creation (32:1-6).

Conversation (4 C)

When the people observe Baruch departing from them after his speech (32:8), they assume that he is leaving them permanently. They react with panic (32:9-33:3). Accusing Baruch of forsaking them like a father his orphan children, they lament that death would be preferable to life without him. Moreover, they assert that Baruch's departure contradicts Jeremiah's instructions to him. The conversation between Baruch and his people concludes as Baruch assures them that he is leaving them only temporarily to return to the Temple and seek further enlightenment (34:1).

This lengthy encounter between Baruch and his people is the first of its kind in the book. Striking structural similarities between this segment and the encounter between Baruch and God in Block 1 (1 A and

---

[12]After the destruction, Baruch's encounters with his people always occur outside Jerusalem, either in the Kidron valley or in an unspecified location.

B—1:1-5:4) indicate that Baruch's initial reaction to the announcement of
the Temple's destruction is a model for his community's reaction to his
departure from them. Both texts begin with a narrative introduction
followed by a message which announces a forthcoming disaster (1 A and
B—chap. 1; 31:1-32:7).[13] There is a death-wish both in Baruch's reaction
to God's words to him and in the people's reaction to Baruch's departure
from them—Baruch's, because he cannot endure the destruction of his
"mother" (1 B—3:1-2); and his people's, because they cannot envision life
without the guidance of their "father" (32:9-33:3). In each text, the
conversation between the protagonists introduces a question or questions
regarding the appropriateness of what is happening (1 B—3:4-9; 1 B—5:1;
33:1-2). Finally, a temporal element is essential to the assurances given
in each segment. God assures Baruch that the destruction and dispersion
are temporary (1 B—4:1; 1 B—5:3), while Baruch assures his people that
his departure from them is temporary (34:1).[14]

Lament (4 D)

Baruch's community recedes from the story as Baruch goes alone to
the Holy of Holies to lament his inability to mourn sufficiently over what
has happened (chap. 35). This lament is his final expression of distress
over the destruction.

Vision (4 E)

After his lament, Baruch falls asleep and sees a vision (chaps. 36-

---

[13]The nature of the disaster is perceived differently in the two
accounts. In the first text, the disaster is the imminent destruction of the
Temple; in the second, it is the tribulations of the final times.

[14]Bogaert (Apocalypse, 1. 58-69) argues that 34:1 concludes Episode
3. He suggests that Episode 4 then begins with the movement of Baruch
to the Holy of Holies. The artificiality of this episode division is evident
in several ways. First, it ignores the changes in location, characters, and
content which occur in 31:1. Secondly, it overlooks the parallel structure
of Chapters 6-20 and 31-43. (See below, pp. 26-27). In this context, it is
striking that while Bogaert asserts that Baruch's movement to the Temple
for his second lament begins an Episode, he does not suggest that Baruch's
movement to the Temple for his first lament (10:5) also indicates the
beginning of a new unit. Thirdly, Bogaert does not appreciate the function of the lament as a reaction to the desolation mentioned in Baruch's
preceding speech to the elders (32:3-4).

37). A vine and fountain approach a great forest and gradually uproot it. Finally, only one cedar tree is left. The vine confronts the cedar and announces its demise. The tree disappears, and a field full of unfading flowers appears.

Prayer (4 F)

Baruch awakes (37:1b) and responds to the vision with a prayer for its interpretation (chap. 38). He states that his obedience to the Torah and wisdom makes him a worthy recipient of the interpretation (38:4).

Conversation (4 G)

As He did previously (3 C—chaps. 22-30), God replies to Baruch's prayer by initiating further conversation with him (chaps. 39-43). The first subject is the interpretation of the vision (chaps. 39-40). Baruch learns that it describes the defeat of Rome[15] and its last wicked leader (the forest and the cedar tree) by the Messiah (the vine and fountain). After the Messiah has convicted and killed the last Roman leader, he will inaugurate an era of peace and fecundity, which will last until the times previously mentioned are fulfilled. Baruch's first lament (2 B—10:6-11:7) was followed by the discourse (2 C—12:1-4) in which he warned Babylon that God's anger would awake against her in its time. His second lament (chap. 35) is followed by the vision (chaps. 36-37) which describes for him what will happen when that anger does awake.

Baruch responds to the interpretation by asking who will be worthy to live in the last times which have just been described (chap. 41). The specific objects of his concern are two groups within Israel: Jews who have withdrawn from the covenant and thrown off the yoke of the Torah, and proselytes. God replies that the past time belongs to Jews who formerly submitted, but then withdrew from the covenant by mingling with the Gentiles.[16] Those Gentiles who choose to associate with Israel will share in the future time promised to the righteous (42:1-6).

---

[15]The forest is described as the fourth kingdom to rule after the fall of Babylon. This four-kingdom model has a biblical precedent in the visions of Daniel 2 and 7. The author of 2 Baruch has adapted that model to describe Rome. Cf. 4 Ezra 11-12.

[16]The phrase "mingled themselves with the seed of mingled peoples" (42:4) probably refers to intermarriage. See Ezra 9:2; cf. Daniel 2:43.

The use of the terms "Torah," "covenant," and "submit" connect this conversation to the conversation between God and Baruch in Block 2 (2 D—chaps. 13-20). In the former discussion, God emphasized the torment awaiting the many Jews who had not followed the example of Moses' submission, but had chosen to sin despite the fact that they had received the Torah and the covenant. In the present conversation, the "sins" of these many Jews is further described as assimilation to the ways of the Gentiles.

As was the case in Block 2 (2 D--20:3-6), God concludes the conversation by exhorting Baruch to retain what he has learned (43:1; cf. 20:3), instructing him to fulfill certain tasks (43:3; cf. 20:5-6), and promising him that he will receive further revelation (43:3; cf. 20:5-6), and promising him that he will receive further revelation (43:3; cf. 20:6).

Conclusion

Several factors disclose that Chapters 31-43 constitute a major block of material. The beginning of a new section is indicated by the departure of Baruch from Mt. Zion and the assembling of the elders in the Kidron valley. Baruch's conversation with all his people introduces the second cycle of the story by establishing an implicit parallel between his initial reaction to the destruction of his "mother" (1 B—chap. 3) and his community's reaction to the departure of their "father" (32:8-33:3). As Baruch reveals his movement toward consolation by speaking cautious words of hope (32:1-2), his community begins to express their grief.

The exhortation, instructions, and promise which conclude God's conversation with Baruch (chap. 43) form a natural ending to the block. The exhortation that Baruch retain what he has learned (43:1) implies that a particular facet of God's revelation to him has been completed. An outline of the material that will follow is provided by the instructions ("go and command your people . . . come to this place and fast seven days") and by the promise ("then I will come to you and speak with you") (43:3). The changes in location, characters, and subject matter with which that section begins also distinguish it from the material which precedes it.

The common subject matter is another factor which demonstrates that Chapters 31-43 comprise one literary whole. The entire section deals with the Torah and the final manifestation of God's justice. In his speech to the elders (31:3-32:7), Baruch acknowledges that the final times will be more turbulent than the present disaster. However, he promises them that the Torah will protect the faithful community in those times. The lament which follows Baruch's encounter with the people (chap. 35) is his

final expression of grief over the present disaster. It is followed by the
vision (chaps. 36-37) which describes the final manifestation of God's
justice against Rome. Baruch's prayer that the vision be interpreted for
him (chap. 38) establishes a formal connection between the vision and the
subsequent conversation (chaps. 39-43), which begins with the interpretation of the vision (chaps. 39-40). At the same time, Baruch's reference to
the Torah in his prayer (38:2, 4) complements his earlier assurance to the
elders that the Torah will protect them (32:1-2). It also provides a foil for
the latter portion of the conversation between God and Baruch (chaps. 41-
42). There Baruch raises questions about the final manifestation of God's
justice to Jews who have chosen to throw off the yoke of the Torah and to
Gentiles who have chosen to be associated with the people of the Torah.

The symmetry between the structure of Chapters 31-43 and the
cluster of sub-units already identified as Block 2 (chaps. 6-20) supports
the designation of both of these sections as blocks of material. The two
blocks can be summarized in parallel columns:

Block 2	Block 4
narrative— destruction observed (6:1-8:2)	*narrative introduction, speech*— destruction set in perspective; Torah introduced as protection (31:1-32:7)
[Block 1—1:2-5:4]	[Baruch's conversation with people—32:8-34:1][17]
lament—call to life to cease because Zion deso- late (10:6-11:7)	*lament*—impossibility of mourning adequately over Zion (chap. 35)
discourse—assertion that God's wrath will awake against Babylon (12:1-4)	*vision*—description of how God's wrath will awake against the "fourth kingdom" (chaps 36-37)

---

[17]This part of Block 4 is not paralleled in Block 2. It introduces the
second cycle of the story by paralleling the people's reaction to Baruch's
departure (4C—32:8-34:1) to Baruch's reaction to the announcement of
the Temple's destruction in Block 1 (1 B—1:2-5:4).

	prayer—petition for interpretation of vision based on attitude toward Torah (chap. 38)
conversation—God's chastening activity; defense of His justice toward Israel; instructions and promise (chaps. 13-20)	*conversation*—application of God's justice to specific groups within Jewish community; instructions and promise (chaps. 39-43)

A comparison of the content of these two blocks clarifies one function of Block 4 within the structure of 2 Baruch. In several particulars, the content of Block 4 reflects the application of themes discussed in Block 2. The vision (chaps. 36-37) describes in visual form how the awakening of God's wrath, announced in the discourse (2 C—12:1-4), will occur. Moreover, the latter portion of the second conversation (chaps. 41-43) applies the general statements about God's justice in the first conversation (2 D—chaps. 14-20) to two specific groups of persons. In several other particulars the themes of Block 4 move beyond those of Block 2. The encounter between Baruch and his people (chaps. 31-34) deals with the survival of the Jewish community after the destruction rather than with the destruction itself (2 A—6:1-8:2). Here the reaction of Baruch's community to his departure is modeled after his reaction to the announcement of the Temple's destruction in Block 1 (chaps. 1-5). Baruch's prayer (chap. 38) is unparalleled in Block 2. However, it is important because it functions as a bridge between the vision and its interpretation.

Thus, as a comparison of Blocks 2 and 4 demonstrates, one function of Block 4 is to apply the general statements of Block 2 to specific events and groups of persons. Another function, evident in the interaction between Baruch and his people (chaps. 31-34), is the introduction of the issue of the survival of the community after Baruch's death. Finally, the emphasis on a proper attitude toward the Torah brings to the forefront a motif which will predominate throughout the remainder of the book.

Block 5—Chapters 44-52

Block 5 consists of a narrative introduction (44:1), a speech by Baruch to his successors (44:2-45:2), a conversation between Baruch and his community (chap. 46), a brief narrative (chap. 47), a prayer (48:2-24), and a conversation between God and Baruch (48:26-52:7).

Narrative and Speech (5 A and B)

The story continues (44:1) as Baruch obeys the first instruction given to him (cf. 43:3) by returning to his people. He selects certain persons and delivers a testamentary speech (44:2-45:2) in which he transfers the leadership of the community from himself to them. He tells them that his death is imminent; they are to remain loyal to the Torah and to carry on the work of instructing the people in the Torah (44:2-3; 45:1). Within the speech, Baruch also shares part of the revelations he has received. He promises his hearers that endurance in the Torah will lead to the sight of the consolation of Zion, and to participation in the eschatological world and time (44:7-15).

Conversation (5 C)

Baruch's successors react with anger and panic to the announcement of his impending death. Accusing God of humiliating them, they ask Baruch how the community can survive without his leadership (46:1-3). Baruch's response to these concerns (46:4-6) emphasizes the responsibility of the entire community to make use of the resources given to it for its survival. After assuring his successors that leadership under the Torah will not cease for Israel (46:4), Baruch exhorts the community to prepare their hearts to obey the Torah and to submit to those persons who are wise and understanding (46:5). If the people do these things, the good things previously described by Baruch will come to them (46:6).[18]

This lengthy encounter between Baruch and his people is the second of its kind in the book. In the previous encounter (4 A-C—chaps. 31-34), the people's reaction to Baruch's temporary departure from them was modelled after Baruch's reaction to the announcement of the Temple's destruction (1 B—1:2-5:4). Similarities between the present encounter and portions of Block 2 (2 A-C—chaps 6-11) indicate that the reaction of Baruch's successors to the announcement of his impending death is modeled after Baruch's reaction to the sight of the destruction of Jerusalem. Both texts begin with a narrative introduction in which Baruch either returns to or leaves Jerusalem (2 A—6:1; 44:1). In the first text (2 A—6:2-8:2), the sight of the destruction is accompanied by visual confir-

---

[18]The shift in audience from Baruch's successors to the entire community is implied by the shift in Baruch's message from teaching the people (chaps. 44-45) to submitting to the teachers (46:5).

mation for Baruch that angels from a transcendent realm have deprived
the enemy of any real claim to victory. However, Baruch's reaction to
the destruction in the form of his lament (2 B—10:6-11:7) indicates that
the sight of the angelic intervention is not sufficient to console him. In
the present text, the announcement of Baruch's impending death is
accompanied by the assurance that there are resources for the faithful
community to survive in this world and to participate in a future, transcendent realm (chaps. 44-45). However, Baruch's successors' angry
reaction to his words (46:1-3) indicates that the promise of participation
in the future world is not sufficient to console them.

Narrative and Prayer (5 D and E)

After dismissing his successors, Baruch obeys the second instruction
given to him (cf. 46:3) by returning to Mt. Zion and fasting for seven days
(chap. 47).[19] The fast is followed by Baruch's third prayer (48:2-24). In
this prayer, Baruch intercedes for the faithful community which he
addressed in the previous segment and confidently affirms that the Torah
is the basis of their continued existence in this world.

Praise of God's power over time and space (48:2-10) is followed by
the petition that God protect and help the few[20] who have submitted to
Him (48:18-19). This group is described further as the nation which God
has chosen (48:20) and as the one named people who have received the one
Torah from the One and who have not mingled with the Gentiles (48:22-
24). Baruch is confident that the Torah will aid and help them.

Conversation (5 F)

God responds to Baruch's prayer by fulfilling His earlier promise to
speak with him again (43:3). This conversation (48:26-52:7) deals first

---

[19]Bogaert (*Apocalypse*, 1. 58-69) argues that Episode 4 concludes at
47:1 with the announcement of Baruch's departure to Hebron and his
seven-day fast. As was the case with his proposal that 34:1 concludes a
unit, the division is artificial because it does not take into account the
relationship of Baruch's encounter with his community (44:1-47:1) to that
which precedes and follows it. Cf. note 14.

[20]The term translated as "few" is z‘wr’. Charles' translation (*APOT*,
2. 505) is "the little ones." As will become evident in Chapter III (see
below, pp. 62-63), the reference to the *few* in this prayer is an elaboration
of the discussion about the *many* and the *few* in chaps. 16-18.

with the final stages of the scenario which will culminate in eschatological judgment against the nations (48:29-41) and then with the eschatological judgment and destiny of the righteous and the wicked (chaps. 49-52). The two parts of the conversation are separated by Baruch's affirmation of the justness of God's judgment against the nations (48:42-47) and by his rhetorical address to the righteous (48:48-50), which anticipates the remainder of the conversation.

God asserts that the nations[21] will be judged on the basis of the Torah, of which only their pride has kept them ignorant. They will be convicted and sentenced to fire (48:38-41).

In reply to Baruch's question about the form of the resurrection bodies (chap. 49), God describes the final judgment which will follow the resurrection (chaps. 50-51). Each person's eschatological destiny will be determined by his/her attitude toward the Torah in this world. The wicked will deteriorate in torment, while the righteous will be exalted and transformed in stages.

Baruch responds in an appropriate way to God's words by declaring that lamentation should be reserved for the final times (52:3). This eschatological perspective predominates in his subsequent rhetorical address to the righteous (52:5-7). After exhorting the righteous to rejoice in suffering rather than paying attention to those who hate them (52:5-6), Baruch concludes: "*Prepare* your souls for that which is kept for you, and *prepare* your souls for the reward which is laid up for you" (52:7).

The double imperative "prepare your souls" combines the two verbs used previously by Baruch to exhort his community to submit to the Torah and its teachers (4 B—32:1; 5 C—46:5). By repeating the verbs in this manner, Baruch emphasizes the eschatological reward awaiting the community which he previously has addressed (4 A-C—chaps. 31-34; 5 A-C—chaps. 44-46) and for whom he has prayed (48:2-24).

Conclusions

Several factors indicate that the conversation between Baruch and God brings to a conclusion a block of material which extends from Chapter 44 to Chapter 52. The activity outlined at the conclusion of the preceding unit (4 G—43:3) has been completed. Baruch has obeyed God's

---

[21]The identification of the recipients of judgment as the nations in 48:39-41 is made on the basis of terminological parallels to earlier discussions regarding the nations. See below, Chapter III, n. 44.

instructions to him to go and command the people (chaps. 44-46) and to return to Mt. Zion for a seven-day fast (47:2). As He promised He would do, God has once again spoken with Baruch (48:26-52:7). Moreover, the material which follows breaks abruptly with this conversation in terms of both structure and content.

The thematic development throughout the related literary sub-units also supports the designation of this section as one block. Baruch exhorts his community to submit to the *Torah* and its *teachers,* and he promises them that ongoing leadership will not be lacking for them (chaps. 44-46). Then he intercedes for this community in prayer (48:2-24), and confidently affirms that the *Torah* is the basis of their continued exis-tence in this world. The description of the final judgment in the sub-sequent conversation (48:26-52:7) gives a preview of the eschatological exaltation which the faithful will enjoy because they have submitted to the *Torah* and its *teachers* in this world.

The symmetry between the structure of Chapters 44-52 and the cluster of literary sub-units already identified as Block 3 (chaps. 21-30) reinforces the designation of both of these literary wholes as blocks of material. The two blocks can be summarized in parallel columns:

Block 3	*Block 5*
[Block 2—*narrative, lament, discourse* (chaps. 6-11)]	[*narrative, speech, conversation*—Baruch transfers leadership; promises leadership under Torah will continue (chaps. 44-46)][22]
narrative—Baruch sancti-fies self and fasts seven days (21:1-3)	*narrative*—Baruch fasts seven days (chap. 47)
prayer—petition to God to act immediately against nations for sake of His name and people (21:4-25)	*prayer*—intercession for God's faithful people; Torah as basis of continued existence (48:2-24)

---

[22]This part of Block 5 is not paralleled in Block 3. It continues the second cycle of the story by paralleling the people's reaction to the announcement of Baruch's death (chap. 46) to Baruch's reaction to the sight of the destruction (2 A-C—chaps. 6-11).

conversation—present
disaster set in context of
God's overall plan for mankind (chaps. 22-30)

conversation—eschatological destiny of nations described; eschatological destinies of wicked and
righteous described; Torah as
criterion of judgment (48:26-52:7)

The parallelism between these blocks is further illustrated by the fact
that they both follow an outline provided by the instructions and promise
given to Baruch at the conclusion of the preceding blocks.

A comparison of the content of the two blocks clarifies one function of Block 5 within the structure of 2 Baruch. It explicates what was
said in Block 3 about Israel, the nations, and the culmination of God's
plan. The prayer in Block 5 (48:2-24) contains Baruch's intercession for
the faithful Jews who were identified as God's people in the prayer of
Block 3 (3 B—21:4-25). The description of judgment against the nations in
Block 5 (48:29-41) is a response to the substance of Baruch's petition in his
prayer in Block 3 (3 B—21:4-25). God assures Baruch that He will show
His power to the nations at the final judgment; He adds that the Torah
will be the criterion of judgment against them. The description of the
final judgment of the righteous and wicked (chaps. 50-51) completes the
revelation given to Baruch in his conversation with God in Block 3 (3 C—
chaps. 22-30); God describes in detail the judgment which will bring to a
culmination His plan for mankind. As He does so, He emphasizes the
relationship between an individual's attitude toward the Torah and his/her
eschatological destiny.

Thus, as a comparison of Blocks 3 and 5 demonstrates, one function
of Block 5 is to explicate what has been said in Block 3. Another function, evident in the interaction between Baruch and his community (chaps.
44-46), is the development of the issue of the survival of the community
after Baruch's death.

The section of text identified as Block 5 brings to a resolution the
issues which have troubled Baruch and his community throughout the
book. Baruch's acceptance of this resolution is evident in the manner in
which he reworks the concerns he introduced in Block 1 into clear statements of consolation. He replaces his early query ". . . if You deliver
Your people to those who *hate* us . . ." (1 B—3:5) with an exhortation to
the righteous to rejoice in present suffering rather than paying attention
to the deviation of those who *hate* them (52:6). He substitutes the confident assertion ". . . I will not be silent in celebrating the *praise* kept for
the righteous . . ." (48:49) for his initial question ". . . how shall we speak

Your *praise*? . . ." (1 B—3:6). He answers his question ". . . will the world
return to its nature and the age depart to primeval silence? . . ." (1 B—
3:7) by affirming that this world is moving toward a final judgment in
which the righteous will be given the world to come (48:45-50; 52:1-7).

Essentially, the major concerns of 2 Baruch have been resolved.
Baruch has attained consolation regarding his "mother," and his community has been assured that they have the resources to move from grief
over the loss of their "father" to consolation. This sense of completion is
a final indicator that Chapters 44-52 comprise a block of material.[23]

Block 6—Chapters 53-76

Block 6 consists of a narrative introduction (53:1a), a vision (53:1b-
11), a prayer (chap. 54), a brief narrative (55:1-3), and a conversation
between the angel Ramiel and Baruch (chaps. 55:4-76:4).

Narrative Introduction and Vision (6 A and B)

After the instructions and the promise given to Baruch at the conclusion of Block 4 (4 G) have been fulfilled in Block 5 (5 A-F), Baruch falls
asleep and sees a hitherto unannounced vision (53:1b-11). A cloud with
the likeness of lightning at its top pours down twelve sets of alternating
dark and light waters on the earth. After a final shower of dark waters,
the lightning seizes the cloud, hurls it to the earth, and takes dominion
over the earth.

Prayer (6 C)

Baruch awakes (53:12) and utters his final prayer (chap. 54). The
petition that the vision be interpreted for him (54:6, 20) is surrounded by
affirmations regarding the consolation of the righteous and the condemnation of the wicked. Baruch praises God for giving revelatory knowledge

---

[23]Bogaert (*Apocalypse*, 1. 58-69) concurs that the fifth unit of the
book concludes at 52:7. He states that the division between the fifth and
sixth episodes is the most difficult to ascertain. His rationale for the
division is the change in perspectives; the discussion on the resurrection
(chaps. 49-52) and the content of the vision (53:1b-11) have nothing in
common with each other. In this instance, Bogaert has assessed the
situation correctly. However, he fails to realize the importance of the
structural pattern as well as of content.

about the future to those persons who have submitted to Him and His Torah, and he affirms that such knowledge results in consolation (54:4-5). Then he reverses his earlier laments (2 B—10:6-11:7; 4 D—chap. 35) by uttering a lengthy doxology (54:7ff.). The same Baruch who once summoned life to cease because of the "desolation of this mother" (2 B—10:6-11:7) now affirms "blessed be my mother among those who bear . . ." (54:10). This praise of God culminates in a definitive vindication of God's justice and power (54:11-15). Twice Baruch reiterates the responsibility of the individual for his/her decision vis-à-vis God (54:15, 19). Those persons who do not love the Torah or submit to God's power will justly perish (54:11-15). Conversely, those persons who are faithful will receive a reward (54:16).

A rhetorical address to the wicked within the prayer (54:17-18) reiterates the condemnation awaiting them. The exhortation to them to turn to destruction is the converse of the earlier exhortation to the righteous to prepare for their eschatological reward (5 F—52:6-7).

Narrative and Conversation (6 D and E)

After his prayer, Baruch contemplates the condemnation which awaits the wicked (55:1-2). Suddenly, the angel Ramiel appears (55:3) and initiates a conversation with him (55:4-76:4). After chiding Baruch for being troubled by the thought of future torment (55:4-8), Ramiel announces that he has been sent to fulfill Baruch's petition (54:6, 20) by interpreting the vision for him.

The interpretation of the vision (chaps. 56-74) explicates God's general plan for mankind (cf. 3 C—chaps. 22-30) in regard to the specific details of Israel's history. The cloud represents the duration of the world. The bright and dark waters which rained upon the earth reflect high and low points in Israel's history. The sins described in the dark waters frequently include idolatry and other cultic abominations (chaps. 60, 62, 64-65). The bright waters focus on Jewish heroes and their relationship to the Torah and/or Zion (chaps. 57, 59, 61, 63, 66, 68). The dark waters after the twelve sets of waters (chaps. 69-71) are the final turbulent times. They will be followed by the appearance of the Messiah (the lightning) (chaps. 72-74). He will judge the nations and will inaugurate an era of peace and prosperity in which the curses brought about by Adam's sin (56:6) will be reversed.

Baruch's response to Ramiel's words is a doxology (chap. 75). His earlier frustration over God's incomprehensibility (2 D—14:8-19) dissolves into praise of God's goodness and mercy (75:1-6). However, the doxology is not Baruch's final word. He returns to the covenantal imagery of Blocks 2, 4, and 5 in order to make a statement addressed rhetorically to his community (75:7-8). He promises them that if they know from where they have come and submit to Him who led them out of Egypt, they will be able to remember what has happened and to rejoice. If not, they will continue to experience grief over what has happened. Thus, a joyous future resolution of present grief is based on knowledge of Israel's past and submission to the God of the covenant.

The conversation concludes (chap. 76) as Ramiel announces that after forty days Baruch will be taken from the earth. He instructs Baruch to use the interim period to instruct the people so that they might learn to live at the last times.

Conclusion

Several factors indicate that Chapters 53-76 constitute a major block of material. The vision (53:1b-11) breaks abruptly with the conversation which precedes it (48:26-52:7) in structure and in content. Different from the previous blocks, there is no parallelism between the structure of this and another block. However, the section is held together formally by the pattern of vision, prayer, and a conversation which begins with the interpretation of the vision. This conversation concludes with instructions similar to those which mark the end of Blocks 2 (2 D—20:3-6) and 4 (4 G—chap. 43). Moreover, the material which follows the conversation is distinguished form that which precedes it by changes in geography, characters, and content.

The subject matter of Chapters 53-76 also identifies this text as one block of material. This block explicates in three ways the justice and power of God: (1) through Baruch's praise of God's justice and power (the prayer—chap. 54); (2) through the application of God's general plan for mankind to the details of Israel's history (the vision and its interpretation —53:1b-11; chaps. 56-74); and (3) through Baruch's doxology and exhortation to his people (chap. 75).

The function of this block is twofold. It reiterates the motifs of consolation and condemnation as developed in Blocks 1-5, and balances the word of consolation with which Block 5 ends (5 F—52:6-7) with an equally strong word of condemnation to the wicked (54:17-18). It also identifies knowledge of Israel's past and submission to the God of the convenant as the basis upon which the community's consolation depends.

Block 7—Chapter 77

Block 7 consists of a narrative introduction (77:1), Baruch's speech to his community (77:2-10), a conversation between Baruch and his community (77:11-17), and a narrative conclusion (77:18-26).

Narrative Introduction and Speech (7 A and B)

The story resumes as Baruch leaves Mt. Zion and obeys Ramiel's instructions (cf. 76:4) by assembling all the people to speak to them (77:1). In this final speech, Baruch reminds the people that the dispersions of the northern and southern tribes and the destruction of Jerusalem were God's reaction to their sins. He also assures them that if they direct their ways properly their dispersed brothers will come to them (77:2-6, 8-10). He grounds this assurance in an affirmation of God's mercy, grace, and truth (77:7).

Conversation (7 C)

All the people react to Baruch's message by affirming that they will remember the good things of God as best they can (77:11). They also ask that before he dies Baruch write a letter of instruction and a scroll of good tidings to strengthen the brothers in Babylon (77:12). The ground of their request is their perception that all their leaders except Baruch have died (77:13-14). In response, Baruch assures them that the faithful community will never lack leadership because the Torah, which spawns its own teachers, endures forever (77:15-16). Then he agrees to write the letter to the brothers in Babylon and announces that he will send a similar letter to the nine and one-half tribes (77:17).

Narrative Conclusion (7 D)

As required by the story, Baruch leaves the people for a final time (77:18). He goes alone to a tree, writes the two letters, and sends them.[24] The letter to Babylon is sent by men, while the letter to the nine and one-half tribes is transported by an eagle (77:19-26).

---

[24]Baruch's movement to the oak tree emphasizes the sense of finality. He does not return to Mt. Zion, the scene of all of God's revelations to him.

Conclusion

Chapter 77 is designated as a block of material because it essentially forms an epilogue to 2 Baruch. The message of the book has been concluded. Here Baruch delivers that message in the form of a testament and leaves the people for a final time. He reiterates both the people's responsibility for the disaster and also the promise that leadership under the Torah never will be lacking to the faithful community.

The symmetry between this text and the material already identified as Block 1 supports the designation of both these sections as blocks of material. The two blocks can be summarized in parallel columns:

Block 1	Block 7
narrative introduction— the Word of God comes to Baruch (1:1)	*narrative introduction*—Baruch goes to the people (77:1)
conversation—God explains reasons for destruction/dispersion; assures will be temporary (1:2-4)	*speech*—Baruch reiterates reasons for destruction/dispersion; assures will be temporary (77:2-10)
—Baruch raises questions regarding implications of destruction; receives initial assurances from God (3:1-5:4)	*conversation*—the people reiterate crisis caused by leadership vacuum after destruction; receive final assurance and statement of basis of survival from Baruch (77:11-17)
narrative conclusion— Baruch gathers honorable men and shares revelation (5:5-7)	*narrative conclusion*—Baruch writes letters, thereby sharing revelations with diaspora (77:18-26)

2 Baruch began with God's revelation to Baruch; it concludes with Baruch's final revelation to his people. The audience to whom the revelation applies is expanded from the honorable Jews of Jerusalem (1 C, 5:5-7) to all Jews everywhere (77:18-26).[25]

CONCLUSION

2 Baruch is a coherent, artistic composition which tells a story in which Baruch and then his community move from grief to consolation. The story is the key to the structure of 2 Baruch. Its continuity is to be found in the sections of narrative prose. The non-narrative sections of the book are subsumed under the narrative frame by means of narrative introductions in the past tense. The author clusters and arranges the narrative and non-narrative sections as sub-units of larger blocks of material. Each block forms a constituent part of the whole and develops some facet of the issues under consideration. In this way, the story moves from its beginning to its logical conclusion.

On the basis of the preceding analysis of the structure of 2 Baruch, it is now possible to identify the primary issues of the book. They are as follows: the vindication of God as just and powerful in the wake of the destruction; and the survival of the faithful Jewish community in the aftermath of the destruction.

The issue of God's justice and power is raised and resolved in the context of Baruch's private interaction with God. Despite the fact that the Temple has been destroyed, this interaction always takes place in the Temple area. In his private conversations with God, Baruch probes the appropriateness of the destruction in terms of its relationship to God's justice toward Israel and the nations and to His power over the nations. His probing of the theological ramifications of the destruction culminates in his aknowledgment that God's justice and power are effective in the present world but will be manifest openly only on an eschatological level.

The issue of the survival of the faithful Jewish community is raised and resolved primarily in Baruch's public encounters with his people. In these public encounters, which always occur outside of Jerusalem, the people express their fear that the community will not be able to survive without his leadership. In response, Baruch applies the revelation he has

---

[25]Bogaert (*Apocalypse*, 1. 58-69) argues that Episode 6 concludes at 77:17, and that Episode 7 then is composed of 77:18-87:1. The division at 77:17 ignores the break in structure and content which occurs at 76:4. The final division assumes that the *Epistle of Baruch* (chaps. 78-87) is part of 2 Baruch. The analysis of the structure of 2 Baruch in this chapter has demonstrated that the story of 2 Baruch ends at 77:26. The analysis of the content of the book in the following chapter will indicate that the 77:26 terminus of the book can be demonstrated on the basis of content as well as of structure.

received to their practical needs. He promises them that leaders will arise to replace him, and he assures them that, despite appearances to the contrary, God's covenant with them remains in effect. The Torah is the basis of their continued existence in this world, and the key to their entrance into the future world and time.

The narrative conclusion (77:18-26) leaves open-ended the exact identity of the leaders who will succeed Baruch and the structural organization of the community they will lead. As required by the story, Baruch leaves the people for a final time. His legacy to his community is the revelation which is recorded in 2 Baruch. The writing of the letters expands the audience to whom the revelation applies to all Jews everywhere. The task of implementing Baruch's legacy belongs to the community which survives his death and to their leaders.

III

Covenant in Crisis:
An Exposition of the Primary Issues
in 2 Baruch

INTRODUCTION

In Chapter II, I argued that the key to the literary structure of
2 Baruch is the story which is told through the clustering and arrangement
of the individual literary sub-units into blocks of material. In this chapter, I will use the results of that literary analysis to examine more closely
the primary issues which are raised and resolved in the course of the
story. The examination will show on the basis of content, terminology,
and structure how the blocks of material through which the story unfolds
are related to one another.

The analysis of the literary structure of 2 Baruch revealed that the
primary issues of the book are twofold: the vindication of God as just and
powerful in the wake of the destruction; and the survival of the Jewish
community in the aftermath of the destruction. In my exposition, it will
become clear that both of these issues are part of an argument about
theodicy. At stake is the continued efficacy of the covenant which God
made with His people through Abraham and Moses.

In this chapter, I will trace the development of the primary issues
through the various blocks of material. After I have done so, I will conclude the examination by summarizing how the respective issues are
integrated into the larger argument about theodicy. Then I will compare
the results of my analysis with the examinations of 2 Baruch by R. H.
Charles, P.-M. Bogaert, W. Harnisch, A. C. B. Kolenkow, and A.
Thompson.

Throughout the examination of the primary issues of 2 Baruch, I
will be using similarities in terminology as an important guide to the
development of various themes. I will utilize the terms as they appear in
the Syriac text rather than attempting to retrovert them into Greek or

Hebrew. I am assuming that the Syriac translator was consistent in translating the terms that appeared in the document which he translated.[1]

THE VINDICATION OF GOD AS JUST AND POWERFUL

Introduction

In 2 Baruch, the destruction of the Temple raises the question of God's willingness and ability to keep His promises to His people. Immediately after he has learned that Jerusalem will be destroyed, Baruch begins to raise questions about the implications of the destruction for God's continued relationship to Israel (3:4-9) and for His power over the nations (5:1). The questions are existential rather than theoretical and are accompanied by Baruch's expressions of anguish (3:1-3) and grief (5:1). In His reply to these and other questions, God begins the lengthy process of convincing Baruch that, despite appearances to the contrary, He has not broken His covenant relationship with His people and He will keep His promises to them. He vindicates Himself vis-à-vis Baruch's questions by revealing to Baruch that His justice and power are effective in this world, although they will be manifest only in the eschaton.

In this section, I will trace the development of this issue throughout the book. I will show how this aspect of the argument about theodicy is raised and resolved in the private interactions between God and Baruch. My analysis of the issue is divided into three sub-sections: (1) the vindication of God as just (Blocks 1, 2, 4); (2) the vindication of God as powerful (Blocks 1-3); and the vindication of God as just and powerful (Blocks 5-6). The division is possible because of the actual division of material in the book. In Blocks 1-4 each of the relevant literary sub-units is concerned almost exclusively with either God's justice or His power.[2] In

---

[1]For our purposes, the retroversion of the Syriac text to Greek or Hebrew is of questionable value, due to the difficulties and ambiguities surrounding the process. Since we do not know the original language of 2 Baruch, it is quite possible that a retroversion to Greek would not take us back to the original text. Moreover, an attempt to retrovert from Syriac to Greek to Hebrew poses even more difficulties. Therefore, I have attempted to retrovert terms only in the few instances where the evidence seems to warrant it.

[2]The exception is Block 1, where the conversation between God and Baruch deals with God's justice (1B—1:2-4:6) and His power (1B—5:1-3). However, even here the two parts of the conversation are separated by

Blocks 5-6, the motifs of God's justice and power are integrated with each other in the individual literary sub-units and are therefore understood best when considered in ongoing relationship to each other.

The Vindication of God as Just *(Blocks 1, 2, 4)*

In Blocks 1, 2, and 4, God's explanation of His method of chastening the nations and Israel leads to the discussion about His justice.   The conversations between God and Baruch are the sole format for the development of this issue.

Block 1 (Chapters 1-5)

God's opening words to Baruch (1:2-4) introduce key terms of subsequent discussions about God's justice.   God reveals what will happen imminently and why:

> . . . for this reason [the sins of the two tribes], I bring evil on this city and its inhabitants, and it will be removed from me *for a time* (*ʿd zbnʾ*), and I will scatter this people among the Gentiles that they may do good for the Gentiles.   And My people will be *chastened*, and *the time* (*zbnʾ*) will come when they will seek the *prosperity* of *their times* (*dzbnyhwn*).   (1:4 [4-5 Syr.])

The terms "for a time," "chasten," and "prosperity" will be significant throughout the discussion of God's justice. Here they describe the duration of the destruction and the effect that the resultant dispersion will have on God's people.[3]

Baruch reacts to this announcement by declaring that death would be preferable to the sight of the "evils of my mother" (3:1).[4]   Then he

---

instructions to Baruch to go and do as he has been commanded (1B—4:7). Since this conversation introduces the issues, it is logical that both motifs would be mentioned here.

[3]The perception of the destruction and temporary dispersion as God's reaction to His people's sin is not unique to 2 Baruch.   Cf. Deut. 29-30; Jer 4:16-17; 6:5ff.; 29:1-14; and Ezek 4:4-8; 5:6ff.; 12:7ff.; 15:6ff.

[4]The use of the term "evils" (*byšth*) to describe the punishment befalling Jerusalem (3:1) situates Baruch's statement of anguish within a

raises a series of questions about the implications of the destruction for God's continued relationship to Israel and to the world (chap. 3). In response, God reiterates that the destruction will be temporary and that it will have a chastening function:

> Therefore, this city will be delivered up *for a time* (*lzbn'*). And the people will be chastened *for a time* (*bzbn'*) and the world will not be forgotten. (4:1)

There immediately follows a comparison between the earthly city and its heavenly counterpart (4:2-6). The comparison alludes to the eschaton when God's justice will ultimately be manifest: when Adam sinned, the "real" city and Temple were removed from the historical world.[5]

Block 2 (Chapters 6-20)

Partially in response to Baruch's lament (10:6-11:7), God begins His second conversation with him (chaps. 13-20) by explaining how He administers justice by *chastening* the nations and Israel.[6] He states that retri-

---

covenantal context. In the Scriptures, "evils" is almost a technical term used to describe God's punishment of Israel for their sins against the covenant (e.g., Deut 31:17ff.; Jer 6:19; 11:10ff.; 16:10ff.). See W. Grundmann, *"kakos," TDNT* 3 (1965) 477-78. Cf. below, n. 20.

[5]For a discussion of the reference to the heavenly city, see W. Harnisch, *Verhängnis und Verheißung der Geschichte: Untersuchungen zum Zeit- und Geschichtsverständnis in 4. Buch Esra und in der syr. Baruchapokalypse* (FRLANT 97; Göttingen: Vandenhoeck & Ruprecht, 1969), 110-11.

God describes the heavenly city as "engraved on the palm of My hands" (4:2). This imagery is rooted in Isa 49:16. In response to Zion's fear that God has forgotten her, (49:15), God replies that He cannot forget her. Her walls are always before his eyes; He has engraved them on the palms of His hands. Moreover, Zion will not remain desolate. Her children will return to her (49:16-29). In 2 Baruch, the Isaiah text is adapted to contrast the earthly and heavenly cities. Implicit in the adaptation is the conviction that consolation will be operative on an eschatological level. Cf. Rev 21-22, where the heavenly Jerusalem descends from heaven at the eschaton.

[6]The two literary sub-units (lament and conversation) are connected to each other by the reference to the present prosperity of Babylon/the cities (11:1-2; 13:4). See above, p. 19.

bution will not fall on the prosperous cities and the nations until the *consummation* (13:3). Then, *in its time (bzbnh)*, they will be *chastened* fully for all their sins (13:4-8, 11-13). In contrast, Israel's present chastisement is temporary and will lead to her pardon:

> Therefore He previously had no mercy on His own sons, but punished them as His enemies because they sinned. They were *chastened* then, therefore, that they might be pardoned. (13:9-10)

The contrast between the manner in which God administers justice to the nations and to Israel has antecedents in the Scriptures and in several intertestamental documents. Two such passages are cited by K. Stendahl in his examination of the connection between non-retaliation and hatred in relevant Jewish and Christian texts.[7] 2 Baruch does not deal with the topic of non-retaliation and hatred. However, the pattern isolated by Stendahl has striking affinities to the description of God's chastening activity in 2 Baruch 13. Stendahl observes that Deuteronomy 32:30-36 emphasizes that God both punishes Israel by handing them over to the enemy and also stores up the evil of the enemy to use against them on the day of vengeance:

> How could one man pursue a thousand of them [Israelites]. . . if their Rock had not handed them over? For the enemy have no Rock like ours, in themselves they are mere fools. . . . Their wine is the venom of serpents, the cruel poison of asps; all this I [God] have in reserve, sealed up in My storehouses till the day of punishment and vengeance, till the moment when they slip and fall; for the day of their downfall is near, their doom is fast approaching. The Lord will give His people justice and have compassion on His servants; for He will see that their strength is gone: alone, or defended by his clan, no one is left. (Deut 32:30-36)[8]

He notes a similar pattern in 2 Macc 6:12-16:

---

[7]K. Stendahl, "Hate, Retaliation and Love in 1QS x, 10-17 and Romans 12:19-21," *HTR* 55 (1962) 343-55.

[8]Throughout the dissertation, quotations of texts in the Scriptures and the Apocrypha will be taken from *The New English Bible* (New York: Oxford University Press, 1961).

Now I beg my readers not to be disheartened by these calami-
ties [persecution], but to reflect that such penalties were
inflicted for the discipline of our race and not for its destruction. It is a sign of great kindness that acts of impiety should
not be left alone for long but meet their due recompense at
once. The Lord did not see fit to deal with us as He does with
the other nations: with them He patiently holds His hand
until they have reached the full extent of their sin, but upon
us He inflicted retribution before our sins reached their
height. So He never withdraws His mercy from us; though He
disciplines His people by calamity, He never deserts them.
(6:12-16)

Stendahl argues that in this text God's dual method of chastening the
nations and Israel is part of an argument about a theodicy. The lack of
God's immediate intervention against the enemy is justified on the
grounds that He is allowing the enemy, by their continued sins, to merit a
greater punishment on the day of vengeance. In contrast, His present
punishment of Israel is actually a sign of His mercy.

The pattern which Stendahl isolates in these two texts clarifies the
defense of God's justice in 2 Baruch 13. God chastens His people by
punishing them immediately for their sins so that they might be purified
and pardoned.[9] He delays chastening the nations so that they might merit
a greater punishment on the day when retribution finally falls on them.

This interpretation of God's chastening activity offers a new perspective from which to approach the enigmatic statement in Block 1 (1B—
1:4) that the dispersion will enable the people *to do good* for the Gentiles.[10] In the context of God's manner of chastening the nations, the

---

[9]This conception of chastening as God's temporary punishment of
Israel for her sins occurs also in *Pss. Sol.* 7:8-10; 10:1-4; 18:4-7; and in Wis
12:22. It also is an important motif in Tobit, where God's mercy is
described as releasing His people from scourging (e.g., 11:15). See G.
Nickelsburg, *Jewish Literature Between the Bible and the Mishnah* (Philadelphia: Fortress Press, 1981) 30-35. For a discussion of rabbinic traditions about chastisement, see S. Schechter, *Aspects of Rabbinic Theology*
(New York: Schocken Books, 1961) 309.

[10]If the verb *nṭʾb* is translated as a pael rather than an aphael form,
then the statement should be translated "in order that it shall be well for
the Gentiles." In either case, the implications of the statement remain
the same. For a different interpretation of the phrase, see P.-M. Bogaert,
Apocalypse de Baruch (SC 144-45; Paris: Le Cerf, 1969) 1. 409-13.

phrase "to do good for the Gentiles" possibly implies the kind of conduct which will enable them to commit more sins and thereby to merit a great punishment.

Baruch reacts to God's explanation of His chastening activity by raising two concerns (14:1-7). First he complains that the retribution against the nations will be too late to be of value (14:1-3). The complaint is not discussed further in this conversation, but will be treated in Blocks 3 and 5. It is, however, the first clue that the delay in the administration of God's justice to the nations is perceived as a problem by the author of 2 Baruch.

Baruch asserts that God's decision to exercise His justice by chastening Israel in this way only proves the uselessness of righteousness (14:4-7). This concern provides the basis for the remainder of the conversation. As the discussion progresses, it becomes clear that the matter under consideration is the administration of God's justice to the transgressors and the righteous within the Jewish community.

God attempts to show that righteousness is effective by contrasting the eschatological destinies of the transgressors and the righteous.[11] First He argues that, because they knew when they sinned, transgressors of the Torah will be tormented:

> Man would not have understood (yd‹) My judgment if he had not received the Torah and if I had not instructed him in understanding. But now because he transgressed knowingly (yd‹), therefore, because he knew (yd‹), he will be tormented. (15:5-6)

Then He declares that the righteous will receive justice in the future world:

> As regards what you said about the righteous . . . *this world* (hn’ ‹lm’) is for them a strife and a labor with much trouble;

The tradition recorded in Rom 12:20 is similar to 2 Baruch 1:4. There Paul tells the righteous to do good for their enemies, in order to "heap live coals on their heads." Tob 13:1-8 describes "doing good for the Gentiles" in a more positive light. There, the Jews are exhorted to give a positive witness to their faith even under the conditions of exile.

[11]God formulates this response as a direct reply to Baruch's concluding statement that the world, which was created for man, endures while man departs (14:17-19).

and *that which is to come* (hw dʿtyd) a crown of great glory. (15:7-8)

In Block 1 (1B—chaps. 3-4), God concluded His reply to Baruch's questions about the future of Israel by alluding to the eschaton. Here He concludes His reply to Baruch's question about the apparent futility of righteous by contrasting the punishment of those who knowingly transgress the Torah (15:5-6) with the eschatological reward of the righteous (15:7-8).[12]

Baruch's subsequent complaint that time is too short to acquire the measureless (16:1)[13] is the foil which introduces further clarification of the divisions between the transgressors and the righteous within the Jewish community. God uses the example of the life spans and legacies of Adam and Moses to argue that the shortened life span resulting from Adam's sin does not negate the individual's ability to make his/her decision vis-à-vis God.[14] Baruch's reply gets to the heart of the problem:

> He that lit [i.e., Moses] has taken from the light, and *few* are those who have imitated him. But *many* of those whom he lit have taken from the darkness of Adam and have not taken delight in the light of the lamp. (chap. 18)

At this point, the distinction between the transgressors of the Torah and the righteous has been rephrased in terms of the *many* Jews who have chosen the darkness of Adam, and the *few* Jews who have remained loyal to the Mosaic covenant.

---

[12]For an excellent discussion of this theme, see Harnisch, *Verhängnis*, 182-86.

[13]This complaint (16:1) is an interesting contrast to Baruch's previous complaint (14:1-3) that time is too long for eschatological judgment against the nations to be meaningful. In both instances, "time" forms the basis of Baruch's question: however, the function of the reference in the one text is the opposite of its function in the other text.

[14]The emphasis that Adam's sin brought death and a shortened life span but did not negate personal responsibility recurs in 48:42-47; 54:15, 19. This view contrasts sharply with the conviction of 4 Ezra (i.e., 3:20-22; 7:116-26) that because of Adam's sin man is born with an evil heart which impedes his ability to choose the way of life. See W. Harnisch, *Verhängnis*, 106-19. Cf. *Jub.* 23:9, where the shortened life span is attributed to the generations after the flood. Cf. also Wis 4:10-15, where Enoch's achievements are contrasted with his brief life span. For rabbinic traditions about the effects of Adam's sin, see Schechter, *Aspects*, 188, 235-36.

The distinction between the *many* and the *few* within a discussion of theodicy is not unique to 2 Baruch.[15] It is significant in 2 Baruch 15-18 because it anticipates the question of the identification of Israel: who are those *few* Jews worthy to inherit the future world?[16]

God responds to Baruch's concern about the *many* and the *few* (19:1-3) by paraphrasing Deuteronomy 30:15-20. The stipulations of the covenant are still in effect; the Torah rebukes those who transgress it. Implied in this response is the conviction that the *many* Jews will be appropriately punished for their transgressions.

God brings this discussion to a conclusion by emphasizing a technical term which will be important throughout the book--"the consummation of the times" (*šwlmh . . . dzbn'*). In this instance, He uses the motif of *prosperity* to encourage Baruch to look beyond present suffering to a future, better day:

> . . . it is the *consummation of the times* that should be considered . . . and not the beginning thereof. Because if a man is prospered at the beginning and shamefully entreated[17] in his old age, he forgets all the prosperity he had. And again, if a man is shamefully entreated in his beginning and at the end prospers, he does not remember his shameful entreatment. And again, though each person prospered all the time . . . from the day on which death was decreed against those who transgress, and in his end was destroyed, empty would have been everything. (19:5-8)

Thus, the present shameful treatment of the *few* righteous Jews is temporary, and will be rectified at the *consummation of the times*.

---

[15]For example, the contrast is a major motif in 4 Ezra 3:1-9:25 and in the *Testament of Abraham* 9-14. Both books deal with the question of theodicy.

[16]Paul Hanson (*The Dawn of Apocalyptic* [Philadelphia: Fortress Press, 1975] 46-208) argues convincingly that the concept of salvation and damnation cutting through the heart of the Jewish community originates in 3 Isa (e.g., 63:15-16; 65:8-16; 66:5-6). See also G. Nickelsburg, *Resurrection, Immortality, and Eternal Life in Intertestamental Judaism* (Cambridge: Harvard University Press, 1972) 25.

This conception becomes important in intertestamental Jewish documents in which apocalyptic eschatology is a dominant factor. Cf. *Jub.* 23:16-32; Dan 10-12; *1 Enoch* 90.

[17]Cf. 14:14.

Block 4 (Chapters 31-43)

After a lengthy pause (Block 3—chaps. 21-30), the discussion of God's justice resumes in the conversation between God and Baruch in Block 4 (chaps. 31-43). The first part of the conversation applies God's earlier statements about the final retribution against the nations (2D—chap. 13) to a specific event. Through God's interpretation of the cedar/vine vision (chaps. 39-40), Baruch learns how divine retribution will fall on Rome:[18]

> And it will come to pass when the *time* of its (Rome's) *consummation* (*zbn² dšwlmh*) that it should fall has approached, then the principate of my Messiah will be revealed . . . it will uproot the multitude of its host . . . the last leader . . . will be taken up to Mt. Zion, and my Messiah will convict him of all his wickedness . . . and put him to death, and protect the rest of my people . . . and his principate will last forever, until *the times* (*zbn²*) previously mentioned are fulfilled. (39:7-40:4)

Previously (2D—19:5-8), Baruch was encouraged to anticipate "the consummation" as the time when the present situation of shameful entreatment would end forever. Here the term "consummation" is used to refer to the time when Rome's present prosperity will end forever.[19]

The second part of the conversation (chaps. 41-43) clarifies the nature of the transgressions of the *many* Jews identified in Block 2 (2D—chap. 18). It also contrasts the eschatological destiny of those Jews with that of Gentiles who choose to associate with Israel. Baruch initiates this part of the conversation by raising the general question of who will be worthy to live in the final times (41:1). Then he immediately moves from the general to the specific:

> I see many of Your people who have withdrawn from your

---

[18]The vision of the four kingdoms which will succeed Babylon (chaps. 36-37, 39-40) implicitly identifies Rome as the fourth kingdom. See above, p.24, n. 15.

[19]The use of the term "consummation" in different contexts—e.g., the consummation of the times, the consummation of Rome's time—is not unique to 2 Baruch. For a discussion of various kinds of terminology about the end-times, see M. Stone, *Features of the Eschatology of 4 Ezra* (Harvard Ph.D., 1971) 83-96.

covenant and cast off the yoke of the *Torah.* And others I
have seen who abandoned their emptiness and fled under Your
wings. What will be to them? Or how will the *last times*
(*zbn' 'hry'*) receive them? (41:3-5)

God responds first in general terms: those persons with faith will
receive the good (*ṭbt'*),[20] while those who despise will receive the contrary (42:2). Then He continues in more specific terms:

As for those who before *submitted* and afterwards withdrew
and mingled themselves with the seed of the mingled people,
the *time* of these was the *former* . . . and for those who
before did not know but afterwards knew life and mingled
with the seed of the people which had separated itself, the
time (*zbnh hw*) of these is the *latter.*[21] (42:4-5)

The use of the terms "covenant," "Torah," and "submit" in these two
passages connects this conversation to its counterpart in Block 2 (2D—
chaps. 15-19). In this way, the transgression of the *many* Jews mentioned
in Block 2 (2D—chap. 18) is clarified as assimilation to the ways of the
nations. At the same time, it becomes clear that Baruch's community
includes proselytes, who will share the eschatological destiny of the
faithful Jews.[22]

---

[20]The use of the term "good" (*ṭbt'*) (42:2) situates God's remarks in a
covenantal context. In Deut 30:15, the people's decision regarding the
covenant is described as the choice of "life and good, or death and evil."
The term is also connected to the covenant in Jeremiah, where it sometimes has eschatological connotations (e.g., Jer 32:39ff.). See W. Grundmann, *"agathos,"* TDNT 1 (1964) 13-15; cf. above, n. 4. For another
example of the good/evil parallelism, see *1 Enoch* 98:9.

[21]The text reads "the former." I have followed the logical emendation of Charles, *APOT*, 2. 502.

[22]The meaning of "proselyte" is ambiguous throughout 2 Baruch. It
probably refers either to converts to Judaism or to righteous Gentiles who
have chosen to associate with the Jewish community, but have not actually converted to the Jewish faith. For a discussion of attitudes toward
proselytism in this time period, see J. Rosenbloom, *Conversion to Judaism: From the Biblical Period to the Present* (Cincinnati: Hebrew Union
College Press, 1978) 35-66. Cf. the discussion on "Conversion of the
Gentiles" in G. F. Moore, *Judaism in the First Centuries of the Common
Era* (Cambridge: Harvard University Press, 1927) 1.323-53.

As was the case in Blocks 1 (1B—4:2-6) and 2 (19:4-20:2), God concludes the discussion of His justice on an eschatological note. Previously, He encouraged Baruch to anticipate the *consummation of the times* (19:4-8); here, He states that at the *consummation* the dust will be called to raise up everything it has kept *until its time* (*lzbnh*) (42:7-8).

Summary

In Blocks 1, 2, and 4, a grieving Baruch calls into question the manner in which God chooses to administer His justice. In response, God defends His decision to allow the destruction of Jerusalem and thereby vindicates Himself as just in regard to this particular situation.

In Block 1, Baruch reacts to the announcement of the destruction by raising questions regarding the implications of this event for God's covenant relationship with Israel and for the future of the world. He learns that the destruction and dispersion will be temporary, and that the earthly city is only a shadow of its heavenly counterpart.

In Block 2, God explains that the destruction is part of His method of administering justice by chastening Israel and the nations. As the conversation between God and Baruch progresses, it becomes clear that Baruch's questions regarding the administration of God's justice toward Israel actually address the issue of God's justice toward the *few* righteous and the *many* transgressors within the Jewish community. God emphasizes that the Mosaic covenant retains its efficacy; because they sin knowingly, transgressors of the Torah will be tormented. The final adjudication of God's justice will occur on an eschatological level.

In Block 4, God uses the interpretation of the cedar/vine vision to illustrate for Baruch how His justice will be manifest against Rome. In this way, Baruch gains a preview of the culmination of God's method of chastening the nations. Baruch's subsequent questions clarify the transgression of the *many* Jews who have forfeited the covenant status. God emphasizes that they have forfeited participation in the future, eschatological time. Within this conversation, it also becomes clear that proselytes will share the eschatological destiny of the *few* righteous Jews.

The Vindication of God as Powerful
(Blocks 1-3)

In Blocks 1-3, the dimension of *time* also is essential in the discussion about God's power. A variety of literary sub-units provide the format for the development of this issue.

Block 1 (Chapters 1-5)

In Block 1 (5:1), Baruch expresses his grief over the enemy's imminent triumph over God's city and their boasting before their idols. The destruction calls into question God's power to defend His city. God's immediate response to Baruch's grief sets the tone for subsequent discussions about His power over the nations:

> My name and My glory are *forever* and *ever* (*'lm' dl'lm*); and My judgment will keep its right *in its time* (*bzbnh*).[23] And you will see that the enemy will not overthrow Zion . . . but will be ministers of the Judge *for a time* (*lzbn'*). (5:2-3)

Despite the impending destruction, God's power has not faltered. *For the time*, He is using the enemy for His own purposes; ultimately His judgment will be shown to be just.

Block 2 (Chapters 6-20)

After the Babylonian army has surrounded Jerusalem, Baruch is lifted over the city by a strong wind (6:1-3). He watches angels bury the Temple vessels and set fire to the city walls so that the enemy cannot claim that it was they who overthrew Zion (6:4-8:2; cf. 1B—5:3).[24] The temporal distinctions introduced by God in the preceding conversation (1B—5:2-3) reappear in the words the angel addresses to the earth:

> Earth . . . receive what I commit to you [i.e., Temple vessels], and guard them *until the last times* (*lzbn' 'hry'*), so that when you are ordered you may restore them . . . Jerusalem will be

---

[23]The motif of God acting for the sake of His name and glory is a major theme in Ezekiel's response to the first destruction and dispersion. See the discussion in R. Klein, *Israel in Exile* (Philadelphia: Fortress Press, 1979) 69-96.

[24]The legend of the angels burying the Temple vessels is a variant form of a tradition recorded in 2 Macc 2:4-8; *Bib.Ant.* 26:3-15; the *Par.Jer.* 3:1-11; and *Ant.* 18:61-63 (4,1). The various forms of the legend share a conviction that the vessels will be restored in final times. See the discussions about this legend in G. Nickelsburg, "Narrative Traditions in the *Paraleipomena of Jeremiah* and 2 Baruch," *CBQ* 35 (1973) 60-68; M. Collins, "The Hidden Vessels in Samaritan Traditions," *JSJ* 3 (1972) 97-116.

delivered up *for a time* (*lzbn'*) until it is said that it is restored *forever* (*l'lm*). (6:8-9)

Here God's general statements about *time* (cf. 1B—5:2) are exemplified in a specific instance—the fate of the Temple vessels. Moreover, as we will see below,[25] the angel has used resurrection terminology to describe their burial and eschatological restoration.

After lamenting over the destruction of Zion (10:6-11:7), Baruch, in a discourse (12:1-4), announces what will happen to Babylon *in its time*:

> . . . I will speak against you, O land which is prospering . . . do not expect and hope that *in all times* (*bkl zbn*) you will be prosperous and rejoicing. For *in its time* (*bzbnh*) wrath will *awake* against you, which now in *long-suffering* is held as if by reins. (12:2-4)

This warning to Babylon contains the second specific instance of what will happen when God's judgment keeps its rights *in its time* (cf. 1B—5:2).

The terms "awake" and "long-suffering"[26] have antecedents in the Scriptures and in Jewish tradition. The presence of these terms in the discourse illustrates how the author of 2 Baruch utilizes various themes within the broad spectrum of the Scriptures and tradition in order to convey his message to his readers.

For example, the term "awake" has a long history in Jewish tradition.[27] In the song of Deborah, it is used in reference to holy war in a historical instance: "*Awake, awake,* Deborah; *awake, awake,* lead out the

---

[25]See below, pp. 65-67.

[26]Since Baruch's discourse is preserved in a Greek fragment (see Charles, *APOT*, 2. 487), it is possible to compare the Syriac terms with their Greek equivalents. The Greek word translated as "will awake" is *exypnisthēsetai* and the Greek term for long-suffering is *makrothym[ias]*. This latter word is used in the LXX translation of the Scriptural texts cited below. However, the term for "awake" in those texts is *exegeirou* rather than *exypnisthēsetai*.

[27]The tradition of God "awakening" to do battle against the forces of chaos or in holy war for His people is rooted soundly in the Scriptures. For a discussion of this motif, see F. M. Cross, *Canaanite Myth and Hebrew Epic* (Cambridge: Harvard University Press, 1973) 91-111.

host (to war)" (Judges 5:12).[28] In one of the hymns of Qumran, the term is used to describe the eschatological holy war:

> And then at the time of judgment, the Sword of God shall hasten, and all the sons of His truth shall *awake* to [overthrow] wickedness; and all the sons of wickedness shall be no more. (1QH 6:29)[29]

In Isaiah 51:9ff., the term is used both with holy war connotations and also to describe restoration:

> *Awake, awake,* put on Your strength, O arm of the Lord, *awake* as You did long ago in days gone by. Was it not You who hacked Rahab in pieces . . . so the Lord's people will come back set free, and enter Zion with shouts of triumph, crowned with everlasting joy. . . . (51:9-10)

> *Awake, awake,* rise up Jerusalem. You have drunk from the Lord's hand the cup of his wrath . . . look, I [the Lord] take from your hand the cup of drunkenness, you shall never again drink from the bowl of My wrath, I will give it instead to your tormenters and oppressors . . . (51:17, 22-23)

> *Awake, awake,* put on your strength, O Zion, and put on your loveliest garments, holy city of Jerusalem . . . rise up captive Jerusalem, shake off the dust; loose your neck from the collar that binds it O captive daughter of Zion. (52:1-2)

2 Baruch 12 utilizes the holy war connotations of "awake" to describe the eschatological defeat of Babylon. Like 1QH 6:29 and in contrast to Isaiah 51:9ff., *the discourse* does not connect God's awakening to the restoration of Jerusalem.[30] Moreover, the Isaianic sense of the

---

[28]Cf. Zech 2:13; 9:13, where the prophet states that God has "awakened" from His holy dwelling place, and has "awakened" Zion's sons for battle. The result will be the victory of Judah over her enemies and the restoration of Jerusalem.

[29]Translation by G. Vermes, *The Dead Sea Scrolls in English* (New York: Penguin Books, 1968) 117.

[30]Although the restoration of Jerusalem is not mentioned in the discourse, the author expresses the conviction elsewhere that there will be an eschatological restoration of the Temple vessels. See the interpretation of 6:8-9, below, pp. 65-67.

imminence of God's awakening is lacking.[31]

The term "long-suffering" also has a long history in the Scriptures and tradition. In the Scriptures, God's *long-suffering* is consistently described as His patience toward His people, which leads to their forgiveness despite their sin. For example, in Exodus 34 God prefaces His re-writing of the tablets after the golden calf incident with a description of Himself:

> . . . Yahweh, the Lord, a God compassionate and gracious, *long-suffering*, ever constant and true, maintaining constancy to thousands, forgiving iniquity, rebellion, and sin, and not sweeping the guilty clean away. . . (34:6)[32]

In 2 Maccabees 6:12-16, the term *long-suffering* does not describe God's attitude toward Israel. After exhorting his readers not to be discouraged by the persecutions they are experiencing, the author indicates that God is *long-suffering* toward the nations in order to enable them to increase their guilt:

> The Lord did not see fit to deal with us (Israel) as He does with the other nations; with them He is *long-suffering* until they have reached the full extent of their sins, but upon us He inflicted retribution before our sins reached their height. (6:14-15)

The author of 2 Baruch has used the perception of *long-suffering* which is reflected in 2 Maccabees. God's patience works *against the nations*, rather than *for His people*.[33] It is connected to the manifestation of His power and His justice, rather than to the exercise of His forgiveness.[34]

Baruch's discourse is followed by a conversation (chaps. 13-20) in which the issue of God's justice toward Israel and the nations predomi-

---

[31] For a discussion of the perception of God's imminent redemption in Deutero-Isaiah, see Klein, *Israel*, 97-124.

[32] Cf. Num 14:18; and Neh 9:17.

[33] This is precisely the kind of phenomenon observed by K. Stendahl, "Love Hate . . .". See the discussion of God's chastening activity, above, pp. 44-47.

[34] Cf. Rom 9:22-23, where God's patience works against the Jews (the vessels due for destruction) and for the Gentiles (the vessels which are objects of God's mercy).

nates. However, God's concluding words to Baruch return to the motif of *time*, and, in so doing, anticipate the entire discussion of Block 3:

> . . . I have removed Zion now so that I may hasten and visit the world *in its time* (*bzbnh*) . . . go and sanctify yourself . . . [then] I will command you regarding the *method of the times* (*dwbr' dzbn'*). For they are coming and will not delay. (20:2, 5-6)

Block 3 (Chapters 21-30)

Baruch's first prayer (21:4-25) emphasizes his impatience with the delay in the manifestation of God's power caused by His long-suffering (cf. 2 C—chap. 12; 2 D—14:1-3). The prayer begins with an acknowledgment of God's power over creation and of His knowledge of the *consummation of the times* (*šwlmhwn dzbn'*) (21:4-12). Then Baruch asks:

> *How long* (*'dm' l'mty*) will the corruptible remain, and *how long* (*'dm' l'mty*) will the time of mortals be prospered, and *until what time* (*'d 'yn' zbn'*) will those who transgress in the world be polluted with much wickedness? (21:19)

His impatience culminates in the petition:

> Command therefore in mercy, and do what You said You would, so that Your power might be known to those who think Your *long-suffering* is weakness. And show those who do not know that what happened to us and to our city until now is because of the *long-suffering* of Your power, because on account of Your name You called us a beloved people . . . (21:20-21)

A sense of immediacy also characterizes the conclusion of the prayer. Baruch reminds God how many and how desolate the years since the patriarchs have been (21:24). Referring to God's earlier assurance that the *times* will not delay (cf. 20:6), he then exhorts Him: ". . . and now show Your glory quickly and do not delay what You have promised" (21:25).

In response to Baruch's prayer, God initiates further conversation with him (chaps. 22-30). After describing in general terms His plan for mankind (22:1-24:2), He responds to Baruch's further queries by explaining in detail the events which will occur when *the time awakes* (24:3-30:5; cf. chap. 12).

Initially, God uses examples from everyday life to chide Baruch for his impatience (chap. 22).[35] Then He introduces the temporal boundaries of His plan for mankind:

> . . . when Adam sinned and death was decreed against those who should be born, then the multitude of those who should be born was numbered, and for that number a place was prepared where the living might dwell and the dead might be kept. Before that number is fulfilled, the creature will not live again . . . and Sheol will receive the dead. (23:4-5)[36]

Thus, the final manifestation of God's power cannot occur until the process is completed which began when Adam sinned. Completion here is envisioned in terms of the number of persons who must be born prior to the consummation. God assures Baruch that this time is approaching, as He states: "My *redemption draws near* and is *not* as *far away* as previously" (23:7). Then He describes what will happen when that redemption occurs:

> For behold, the days come and the books will be opened in which are written the sins of all who sin and the treasuries in which the righteousness of the righteous is gathered.[37] For . . . *at that time* (bhw zbn⁾) you will see . . . the *long-suffering* of the Most High, which has been through all generations, who has been *long-suffering* toward all who are born, those who sin and those who are righteous. (24:1-2)

In using the terms "draws near" and "not far away" to describe the

---

[35]This motif also occurs in 4 Ezra (e.g., 4:26-32; 5:42-55). The length of pregnancy is the example used there to illustrate the point. See Harnisch, *Verhängnis*, 270-75, 293-301, 309-16.

[36]The birth of a certain number of souls as a precondition for the consummation appears in several rabbinic traditions. For example, in *b. Yebam.* 62a and 63b and in *b. Nid.* 13b, a discussion about propagation includes the comment: ". . . the Son of David will not come before all the souls in Guf have been disposed of. . . ." Cf. *b. Abod. Zar.* 5a. In contrast, according to 4 Ezra 4:36 the end will not come until the full number of the souls of the righteous is complete.

[37]The description of the final judgment in terms of the "books of sins being opened" probably is an allusion to Dan 7:9-10. There the ancient of days takes his seat, the court sits, and the books are opened.

approach of God's *redemption*, the author is alluding to Isaiah 46-47.
There God's promises that He will carry His people to safety (46:3-4) and
that He will take vengeance against Babylon (chap. 47) include the statement:

> I have a plan to carry out and carry it out I will. Listen to me
> . . . I bring my victory *near*, it is *not far off*, and My deliver-
> ance will not be delayed; I will grant *deliverance* in Zion and
> give my glory to Israel. (46:11-13)

This text, like 2 Baruch 23:7, anticipates redemption and restoration.
However, while the Isaianic text suggests that deliverance is imminent,
the 2 Baruch passage emphasizes that redemption is an eschatological
reality which will occur only after all the steps in God's plan have been
completed.

Baruch is not satisfied by God's explanation of His plan for mankind. His continued anxiety about the delay in the manifestation of God's
power is evident in his statement that he knows neither what will happen
to the enemy nor when God will visit His works (24:3-4). In response, God
describes in detail the final stages in the time-line of His plan. The time
announced by Baruch in his discourse (2C—12:4) will awake *at the end of
days* (*lḥrtᵓ dywmtᵓ*) when the inhabitants of the earth will abandon hope
because of the tribulations they will experience (chap. 25). Twelve episodes of disaster and destruction will comprise the parts *of that time* (*dhw
zbnᵓ* 27:14) (chaps. 26-27).[38]

Further descriptions of the end-times follow. Each description is
characterized by the phrase "at that time" (*bhw zbnᵓ*) (29:2, 8; 30:2). All
the earth will experience the disasters of those times; only the inhabitants
"of this land" will be protected (29:1-2).[39] When the twelve parts of time

---

[38]The concept of the overturning of the normal course of nature
prior to the Messiah's advent almost certainly is rooted in the descriptions
of the classical prophets about the coming of the Day of Yahweh. See J.
Klausner, *The Messianic Idea in Israel* (New York: Macmillan Co., 1955)
237ff. Cf. the appropriations of this tradition in 4 Ezra 5:1-12; *b. Sanh.*
97a; Mark 13:7-8.

[39]The statement that only "the inhabitants of this land" will be protected during the final tribulations seems to be unique in intertestamental
literature to 2 Baruch and to 4 Ezra 12:34. Charles (*APOT*, 2. 497) suggests that the phrase reflects Joel 2:32. According to Joel, there will be
a remnant on Mt. Zion when the Day of Yahweh comes. Cf. 4 Ezra 13:48-

have been completed, the Messiah will be revealed. A time of peace and fecundity will follow, which will be enjoyed by all those persons who have come to the *consummation of the times* (*lšwlmh dzbn*).[40] After the time of the Messiah is fulfilled, he will return and the final stage in the *consummation of the times* will begin:[41]

> Then all who have fallen asleep in hope of him will rise again. And it will come to pass *at that time* (*bhw zbn*) that the treasuries will be opened in which is preserved the souls of the righteous . . . and the first will rejoice and the last will not be grieved. For they will know . . . it is the *consummation of the times* (*šwlmhwn dzbn*). But the souls of the wicked . . . will waste away . . . (30:2-5)

The conversation ends on this eschatological note. God's plan can not be rushed. However, when all the steps have been completed it will culminate in the resurrection of the dead.

Summary

In Blocks 1-3, a grieving Baruch questions God's failure both to avert the destruction and also to show His power to the nations soon after the destruction. In response, God vindicates Himself as powerful by revealing how the city was overthrown and by setting the present disaster within the context of His overall plan for mankind.

In Block 1, God responds to Baruch's fear that the enemy will overthrow the city and boast before their idols by asserting that He is temporarily using the enemies as His ministers.

In Block 2, Baruch receives visual confirmation of God's earlier promise that the enemy would not overthrow the city. In his discourse, he

---

50, where Ezra is told that the Messiah will unite the ten tribes with "the survivors of your own people, who all are found within my sacred boundary" (13:48).

[40]The description of the eschaton as a time of peace and abundance is common. For examples of variations on this theme see Amos 9:9-15; Isa 11:6-9; 65:25; Jer 23:5-6; Joel 3:18; *Jub.* 23:26-31; *T. Levi* 18:2-6; *1 Enoch* 10:17-19.

[41]The distinction between the time of the Messiah and the final times is not at all unique to 2 Baruch. Cf. 4 Ezra 7:26-36; *b. Sanh.* 99a. For a discussion of various traditions about the relationship of the Messianic era to the final times, see Klausner, *Messianic Idea*, 408-26.

warns Babylon that God's power, now restrained by long-suffering, will awake against her at the proper time.

In Block 3, Baruch expresses His impatience with God's slowness, and he petitions God to show His power to the nations immediately. In response, God describes His plan for mankind, which must run its course before the end can come. The present time is only one segment in a broad scenario, which extends from the creation to the consummation.

The discussion in Block 3 helps to clarify the meaning of "eschatology" in 2 Baruch. History is a process which has a beginning and an end. When that process has been completed, God will intervene and initiate the events which will comprise the "consummation of the times." The culmination of this intervention will be the resurrection and final judgment.

The Vindication of God as Just and Powerful
(Blocks 5-6)

In Blocks 5-6, the themes of God's justice and power become integrated with one another within the individual literary sub-units. The result is a resounding vindication of God as just and powerful in His dealings with Israel and the world. On the basis of this vindication, Baruch can exhort the faithful community to remain loyal to its Mosaic heritage.

Block 5 (Chapters 44-52)

In Block 5, the theme of God's power over time and space provides the framework for the integration of motifs developed in earlier discussions of God's justice and power. The purpose of this integration is twofold. (1) It makes explicit the characteristics which define the faithful community as "Israel," and it emphasizes that the Torah protects that faithful community in this world. (2) It provides the basis for a description of the final judgment and the eschatological destinies of the righteous and wicked. Secure in his knowledge about *the future,* Baruch is able to acknowledge that God is just and powerful even in *the present time* and to exhort the righteous to share his perspective. The contexts in which the integration of previous motifs occur are a prayer (48:2-24) and God's final conversation with Baruch (48:26-52:7).

The prayer begins with an acknowledgment of God's power over time and space (48:2-10; cf. 3B—21:4-12). After using the idea of the *shortness of this time* (qlyl zbn³) to contrast God's eternity and power with His creatures' mortality and powerlessness (48:12-17), Baruch petitions;

> Protect us in Your mercy and in Your compassion help us . . .
> behold the *few* (z'wr') who have *submitted* to You and save all
> who draw near to You . . . and *cut not short* the *time* (zbn') of
> our aid. (48:18-19)

In his first prayer (3B—21:4-25), Baruch petitioned God to show His power
to the nations by initiating the *final times* immediately. Here he petitions
God to show His power by protecting the community which is faithful to
Him in the *present times*. The use of the phrases "cut not short the
times" and "the few who have submitted" connect this petition to the
conversation between God and Baruch in Block 2 (2D—chaps. 14-20).
There the phrases were used with reference to Moses and to those Jews
who remained loyal to the covenant he instituted. Although he knew his
time was *short* (dzbnh qlyl) (19:2), Moses *submitted* to his Creator and
instituted the covenant of life and death. He has been imitated by only a
few (qlyl) Jews (17:4-19:3). The application of these phrases to Baruch's
community defines that community as the minority of Jews and the
proselytes[42] who have remained loyal to the heritage of Moses.

    Baruch's subsequent words develop further the identity of this
faithful minority. By stating "this is the people You have chosen and the
people to whom You find no equal" (48:20), Baruch returns to the terminology of his first prayer (3B—21:4-25). There he used the phrase "a
beloved people" (3B—21:21) to describe all Israel in contrast to the
nations. The use of this kind of terminology to describe the community
for whom Baruch prays is an indication that he defines this faithful minority as "Israel."

    The final part of the prayer elaborates the description of the
community and asserts that the Torah is the basis of their survival in the
present time:

> In You do we trust,[43] for Your Torah is with us, and we know
> we will not fall as long as we keep Your covenant. *In all
> times (bklzbn)* we are blessed because we have not mingled

---

[42]The phrase ". . . and save those who draw near to You . . ." (48:19)
was used earlier to describe proselytes (4G—42:3). This phrase sometimes
has cultic significance in the Scriptures (e.g., Exod 3:5, Lev 21:21). Thus,
its presence is not surprising here. See H. Preisker, "engys," *TDNT* 2
(1964) 330-32.

[43]Cf. 14:12. Like their ancestors, Baruch's community can continue
to trust God's promises.

with the nations. We are one named people who have received one Torah from the One: and the Torah . . . will aid
us, and . . . wisdom . . . will help us. (48:22-24)

The description of the community in this prayer must be read
against the backdrop of the description of the *many* in the conversation of
Block 4 (4G—chaps. 41-42): the *few* have kept the covenant (48:22) rather
than withdrawing from it (41:3; 42:4); they base their trust on the presence of the Torah among them (48:22) rather than throwing off the yoke
of the Torah (41:3); unlike the Jews mentioned in 42:4, they have not
mingled with the Gentiles (48:23). Therefore they are Israel, and Baruch
is confident that obedience to the Torah insures their survival in this
world (48:24).

In contrast to the prayer's emphasis on *this time,* the conversation
which follows (48:26-52:7) integrates the themes of God's justice and
power in order to describe the eschatological judgment at *the end of
time.* Because of the new perspective he gains, Baruch is able to affirm
that God is just and powerful in *the present time.*

The initial part of the conversation (48:29-47) describes God's
eschatological judgment against the nations.[44] As in the description of
the final times in Block 3 (3C—chaps. 25-30), so here the beginning of the
end is portrayed as a time of disaster and destruction (48:31-37). In Block
3, the phrase "at that time" delineated the final steps in God's plan—the
tribulations, Messianic era of peace and fecundity, and the resurrection
(3C—chaps. 29-30). Here it appears within a statement regarding the
scarcity of wisdom *at that time* (48:33, 36), and it introduces the topic of
the final judgment against the nations (48:38).[45] The charges against the
peoples of the earth include the following:

---

[44]The text does not refer explicitly to the nations. However, the
terms used to describe the recipients of judgment are borrowed from
earlier segments which deal with the nations. The statement ". . . has not
remembered my beneficence" (48:29) is strikingly similar to God's
indictment of the nations (". . . have denied My beneficence") (2D—
13:12). The reference to "long-suffering" has antecedents in Baruch's
discourse against Babylon (2C—12:4) and in his prayer that God show His
power to the nations (3B—21:21).

[45]The differences in terminology, the order of events, and the
emphases indicate that the author is using different traditions about the
final times in Blocks 3 and 5. For a discussion of this practice, see above,
pp. 5-6. Cf. M. Stone, *Features,* 44-215.

> . . . *in all those times* (*bkwlhwn hlyn zbn*ʾ) they polluted
> themselves, and they overreached. Each man walked in his
> own works, and did not remember the Torah of the Mighty
> One . . . each of the inhabitants of the earth knew when he
> was transgressing, but my Torah they did not know because of
> their pride. (48:38, 40)

All the peoples of the earth will be judged by the Torah. Because they
knew when they transgressed, they will be punished (48:38-39).[46]

In Block 3, the detailed prospectus of the final times (3C—chaps.
25-30) was prefaced by a general description of the manifestation of God's
power through His plan for mankind (3C—chaps. 22-23). In Block 5,
Baruch responds to what God has just said about the final times of the
nations by acknowledging the justness of God's plan for mankind:[47]

> . . . You [God]commanded the dust to produce Adam and You
> know the number of those who are born from him, and how
> much they have sinned . . . their end will convict them and
> Your Torah, which they have transgressed, will requite them
> on Your day. (48:46-47)

Baruch's impatience has been allayed because now he can view the present
from the perspective of the final times.

This perspective dominates the words with which Baruch interrupts
his conversation with God to address the righteous:

> . . . surely, as in *a short time* (*dbzbn*ʾ *qlyl*) in this world which
> passes away you have endured much labor, so in that world to
> which there is no end you will receive great light. (48:50)

---

[46]The theme of final eschatological judgment against the nations
occurs frequently in intertestamental literature. However, the statement
that the Torah will be the criterion of judgment against them is not
common. The closest parallel to 2 Baruch 48:38, 40 is 4 Ezra 13:25-38.
There the Messiah destroys the nations by the Torah, which is represented
by flame flowing out of his mouth. Cf. the discussion of rabbinic
traditions about commands binding on all mankind in Moore, *Judaism*, 1.
274-80.

[47]The rhetorical question (48:42) with which Baruch begins his comments ("Oh, Adam what have you done . . .?") directs the reader back to
God's words in Chapter 23.

Basically, Baruch is repeating to the righteous what God revealed to him in 15:7-8 (2D).

The technique of interjecting a direct address out of context also appeared in Baruch's first lament (2B—10:6-11:7). Baruch's address to Babylon with the lament (11:1-2) anticipated the discourse against Babylon (2C—12:1-4) which followed the lament. Similarly, Baruch's address to the righteous within this conversation with God anticipates the subject matter of the remainder of the conversation (chaps. 49-52).

The final segment of the conversation deals with the eschatological destinies of the righteous and the wicked. In response to Baruch's questions about the shape of the resurrection bodies (49:2-3), God declares:

> . . . the earth then will restore the dead, which it now receives (*dmqbl*ᵓ) to preserve (*dttr*) them . . . as it has received them, it will restore them, and as I delivered (*d*ᵓ*šlmt*) them unto it, so shall it raise (*mqym*ᵓ) them. (50:2)

The terminology previously used to describe the burial and ultimate restoration of the Temple vessels (2A—6:8-9)[48] here is used to describe the burial and resurrection of the dead.[49] The use of this terminology in these two instances is an example of the integration of both facets of God's vindication of Himself. All challenges that God was impotent to stop the destruction of Zion will be proved false at the eschatological time when Jerusalem is restored. Similarly, all challenges that God is unjust in His dealings with the wicked and righteous will be negated at the eschatological judgment which will follow the resurrection.

The details of that eschatological judgment are the subject of the remainder of God's comments (chap. 51). The individual's eschatological destiny will be determined by his/her attitude toward the Torah in this

---

[48]The text describing the burial of the Temple vessels reads: "Earth . . . receive (*qbl*) these things which I commit to you, and preserve (*ntr*) them until the last times . . . Jerusalem will be delivered up (*tštlm*) for a time, until it is said that it is raised (*ttqn*) forever." (6:8-9)

[49]This is a fixed terminology which is used in several intertestamental documents to describe the resurrection of the dead—e.g., *1 Enoch* 51:1; *Bib. Ant.* 3:10; and 4 Ezra 7:26-38. For a discussion of resurrection terminology, see H. Cavallin, *Life After Death* (ConBNT 7:1; Lund: CWK Gleerup, 1974) 44, 74-80. Interestingly, only 2 Baruch uses this terminology to establish a parallel between the restoration of the Temple vessels and the resurrection of the dead.

world.[50] The description of the exaltation of the righteous (51:7-14)[51] includes motifs originally appearing in God's comments about the heavenly city (4:2-6) and in Baruch's first lament (10:17). In Block 1 (4:2-6), God assured Baruch that the earthly Jerusalem was only a shadow of its heavenly counterpart which, along with Paradise, was removed from the earth when Adam sinned. In Block 5, God states that the righteous will enter the time and world now hidden from them, and will see Paradise and the divine throne (51:7-11). In his first lament (10:6-11:7), Baruch's grief over the desolation of Zion included the exhortation "speak no more of beauty (šwpr³) . . . or loveliness (y³ywt³)" (10:17). Now, in his final conversation with Baruch, God describes the exaltation of the righteous: ". . . and they shall be changed into every form they desire, from beauty (šwpr³) to loveliness (ly³ywt³) . . ." (51:10). The use of this language continues the parallelism with which this portion of the conversation began (50:2). The Temple vessels and the righteous dead will remain in the earth until God's plan culminates in the final judgment. Then both will be raised.[52]

The element of *time* remains essential in God's concluding remarks. The righteous have chosen the time which will not age them, and in which they will be delivered from the world of tribulation (51:8-14). Those persons who will perish (51:16) have not chosen *this time* (zbn³ hn³): they have selected *that time* (zbn³ hw) whose limits are full of groans and lamentations. In these remarks, God contrasts "present" and "future" time in a different way than He did before. Previously, when defending His justice and power in regard to the destruction, God distinguished between *this (present) time* and *that (future) time*. Here, when He describes the eschatological judgment, *this time* refers to the *future time* of the righteous, and *that time* to the *past time* of the wicked. This is an indication of the changed orientation in this conversation. Previously, discussions about the present time led to statements about the future time; here, discussion about the future time leads to a statement about the present time.

Baruch's response to God's description of the eschatological judg-

---

[50]See Harnisch, *Verhängnis*, 182-93.

[51]See G. Nickelsburg, *Resurrection*, 84-85. He discusses the juxtaposition of vindication and exaltation motifs in this description. Nickelsburg notes that 2 Baruch 51 testifies to the development of the exaltation scene of Wis 4:20ff. into a scene of judgment. Cf. *1 Enoch* 62-63.

[52]Although it is not stated explicitly, it appears that at the consummation the Temple vessels will be placed in the heavenly Temple, and the righteous will be taken into the heavenly world.

ment emphasizes further his recognition that the future time offers the best perspective from which to approach the present time. His statement that lamentations should be reserved for the future torment (52:3) implies that lamentations over the present desolation (cf. 10:5; chap. 35) should cease. Baruch's second direct address to the righteous encourages them to make his perspective their own:

> . . . rejoice in the suffering which you now suffer: for why do you look to the aberration of those who hate you? Make ready your soul for that which is reserved for you, and prepare your souls for the reward which is laid up for you. (52:6-7)

Secure in his knowledge about the future, Baruch is able to acknowledge that God is just and powerful even in the present time, and to exhort the righteous to share this perspective.

Block 6 (Chapters 53-76)

In the prayer (chap. 54) and the conversation between Ramiel and Baruch (chaps. 55-76), the vindication of God's justice and power is expressed in three ways. (1) The same Baruch who earlier questioned God now praises Him precisely as just and powerful. (2) God's general plan for mankind is applied to the specific details of Israel's history. (3) Baruch speaks a final doxology and delivers a rhetorical exhortation to his community to remain loyal to the covenant.

Baruch's fourth prayer (chap. 54) follows the cloud/waters vision (52:1b-11) and contains Baruch's petitions that the vision be interpreted for him (54:6, 20). The prayer emphasizes the condemnation justly awaiting the wicked and the consolation possible for the righteous through their knowledge of the eschatological future.

As he did in his first (3B—21:4-25) and third (5E—48:2-24) prayers, here Baruch begins with an acknowledgment of God's knowledge and power over time and space (54:1-3). He reiterates the eschatological perspective he has gained by asserting ". . . and against the works of the inhabitants of the earth You hasten the beginning of *the times* (*dzbn*')" (54:1).[53] Then he affirms that consolation is available to the righteous because of God's revelations to them:

---

[53]Cf. 20:1. There God uses the term "hasten" to assure Baruch that the consummation is approaching.

> You who reveal to those who fear You what is prepared for
> them, so that they may be consoled ... and [You] reveal what
> is hidden to the pure, who in *faith* have *submitted* to You and
> Your Torah. (54:4-5)

The use of the terms "faith" and "submit" connects this passage to the
conversations between God and Baruch about the righteous and wicked
within Israel (2D—17:1-19:3; 4G—chaps. 41-43) and to Baruch's intercession for his community (5E—48:19). In this way, the recipients of God's
revelatory consolation are identified as the *few* Jews and the proselytes
who have remained loyal to their Mosaic heritage and who therefore
represent "Israel."

The lengthy doxology which follows Baruch's petition (54:7ff.)
culminates in Baruch's most elaborate vindication of God as just and
powerful:

> For with Your counsel, You govern all the creatures Your
> right hand has created ... and justly do they perish who have
> not loved Your Torah, and the torment of judgment will await
> those who have not submitted to Your power. For though
> Adam sinned and brought untimely death to all, yet of all
> those born from him, each one has prepared for his own soul
> torments to come and each has chosen the glory which is
> prepared. For he who has faith will receive a reward. (54:13-
> 16)

Here Baruch no longer speaks simply about Israel; his words apply to all
mankind. The vindication of God has been expanded from the specific
situation of the destruction to include all of His dealings with mankind.

Baruch interrupts his praise of God in order to speak directly to the
wicked (54:17-18). The exhortation that they turn to destruction because
their just condemnation approaches contrasts sharply with Baruch's earlier
exhortation to the righteous to rejoice in present sufferings in anticipation of their approaching reward (5F—52:7).[54]

---

[54]The address to the wicked is followed by the statement "Adam is
therefore not the cause except of his own soul, but each of us is the Adam
of his soul" (54:19). The statement is redundant (see 54:15). The repetition of the motif of human responsibility despite Adam's sin (cf. also
48:42-47) perhaps is a response to the type of tradition represented by the
Adamic speculation in 4 Ezra. For further discussion, see Harnisch, *Ver-*
hängnis, 194-97. He suggests that the author of 2 Baruch, like that of 4

Baruch concludes the prayer by re-emphasizing condemnation and consolation:

> For at the *consummation of the world* (bšwlmh d‘lm) ven-
> geance will be taken upon those who have done wickedly
> according to their wickedness, and You [God] will glorify the
> *faithful* according to their faithfulness. For those who are
> *among Your own* You govern, and those who sin You blot out
> from *among Your own*. (54:21-22)

Baruch's first prayer ended with an exhortation to God to show His power to the nations immediately (21:24-25); his final prayer concludes with a statement of confidence that God's justice will be manifest at the consummation. This contrast offers a further example of the way in which Baruch's former impatience has been allayed by the revelations he has received.

The use of the term "faithful" in the conclusion of Baruch's prayer reiterates the identification of the people for whom he prays as the *few* Jews who have remained loyal to their Mosaic heritage. This identification helps to explain the phrase "among Your own" in the concluding verse of the prayer (54:22). The target of God's vengeance will be the Jews who have forfeited the status of Israel: God will "blot them out." Conversely, the Jews and proselytes faithful to the covenant will be governed and glorified because they are "among God's own."

After his prayer, Baruch sits under a tree and contemplates the condemnation awaiting sinners (55:1-2). Suddenly, the angel Ramiel appears and initiates a conversation with him (chaps. 55-76). Ramiel chides Baruch for being troubled about the future times (55:4-8) and announces that he has been sent to interpret the vision for him (56:1). There is an interesting contrast between these words and those of God in an earlier conversation with Baruch (3C—chaps. 22-30). In Block 3, God chided Baruch for being troubled because he did not know the end of the times; then He set the present situation within the context of His overall plan and described in detail the final stages of that plan. In Block 6, Ramiel chides Baruch for being troubled because he has learned about the end of the times; then, by announcing that he will interpret the cloud/ waters vision, he sets the stage for the application of God's overall plan to the specific details of Israel's history.

Ezra, is struggling against a type of thought in which personal freedom and responsibility have no place.

Ramiel introduces the interpretation of the vision by stating:

> The Mighty One has made know to you [Baruch] the methods
> of the times that have passed, of those that are destined to
> pass in His world from the beginning of its creation *until its*
> *consummation* (*'dm' lšwlmh*), and of those things which are
> deceit and those which are in truth. (56:2)

Baruch learned about the methods of the times in Blocks 3 and 5. Now he
will learn how Israel's history from the creation to the consummation is
divided into twelve alternating sequences of dark waters (times of deceit)
and bright waters (times of truth).[55]

The vindication of God's justice and power is particularly evident in
two themes: (1) the contrasts between the time of Adam on the one hand
and of Abraham and the Messiah on the other hand; and (2) the importance
of the people's attitude toward the cult throughout Israel's history.

The cycle of grief, birth, and death in the "dark waters" segment
about Adam is countered by a cycle of Torah, future judgment, and a
renewed world in the "bright waters" segment about Abraham:

> [regarding Adam]. . . for when he transgressed, untimely
> death came into being. Grief was *named* (*'štmh*), and anguish
> was prepared. And pain was created, and trouble consum-
> mated, and disease began to be established, and Sheol kept
> demanding to be *renewed* (*dtthdt*) in blood. And the *generat-*
> *ing* (*nsb'*) of children was begun, and the passion of parents
> produced, and the greatness of humanity was humiliated, and
> goodness languished. (56:6)

> [regarding Abraham]. . . the unwritten Torah was *named*
> (*mštmh*) . . . and belief in the coming judgment was *generated*
> (*mtyld'*), and hope of the world that was to be *renewed*
> (*dmthdt*) was built up. (57:2)

---

[55]The imagery of the cloud/waters vision is unique to 2 Baruch.
However, there are other texts which emphasize the periodization of
time, often with alternating cycles of good and evil. An example not too
far removed from 2 Bar 53ff. is the Apocalypse of Weeks (*1 Enoch* 93:1-
10; 91:11-17). According to this text, history is divided into periods of ten
"weeks," in which both righteousness and wickedness are found. However,
unlike 2 Baruch, salvation occurs within the ten-week frame. According
to the cloud/waters vision, the twelve sets of waters will be followed by
another set of dark waters and then by the Messianic era.

As the repetition of these key terms indicates, eschatological hope has been available to God's faithful people since the time of His first contact with Israel.[56]

According to the interpretation of the vision, the travail which has characterized creation since Adam sinned will be reversed in the Messianic era which will follow the final dark waters of tribulation (chaps. 72-74):[57]

> . . . then healing will descend . . . and disease will withdraw, and anguish . . . will pass from among men . . . and no one will die untimely . . . and women will have no more pain when they bear. (73:2-7)

Thus, the history of Israel—and of the world—will culminate in the restoration of creation to its original condition.[58]

The importance of the people's attitude toward the cult is a central theme throughout the exposition of Israel's history. There is a definite correlation between their attitude toward the cult and God's activity on behalf of or against them. For example, references to the cult appear in all the "bright water" segments dealing with Jewish heroes after the time of Abraham.[59] In addition, the building (chap. 61) and rebuilding (chap.

---

[56]The eschatological hope available to Israel throughout her history is elaborated in the bright waters of Moses and those like him (chap. 59). The description of the revelations given to Moses is the most extensive in the interpretation of the vision.

[57]The description of the final turbulent times (chap. 70) emphasizes the overturning of the normal order of nature and the ensuing chaos, as do the descriptions in Block 3 (25:1-29:1) and in Block 5 (48:33-37). The initial statement "behold the days come . . . when the time of the age is ripened and the harvest of its good and evil seeds has come" (70:2) is unparalleled in the remainder of 2 Baruch. The terminology is similar to that of 4 Ezra 4:26-32.

[58]If the texts are read literally, the restoration will be partial because women will continue to bear children in the Messianic era (cf. 56:6, where the generating of children is part of the curses brought about by Adam's sin). However, it is quite possible that the curse of childbearing involves bearing children *in pain*. In this description of the Messianic era, the role of the Messiah continues to be ambiguous. See above, p. 60, n. 41.

[59]E.g., Moses (59), David and Solomon (61), Hezekiah (63), and Josiah (66).

68) of the Temple [60] comprise two of the six "bright waters," while grief over the present desolation of Zion is the topic of the "black eleventh waters" (chap. 67). God's decision to send the northern and southern tribes into captivity and to allow Zion to be uprooted (the "black seventh and ninth waters"—chaps. 62, 64) was based on the cultic sins of His people and their leaders.

The contrast between the times of Hezekiah (chap. 63) and Manasseh (chaps. 64-65) provides a particularly good example of the importance of a proper attitude toward the cult. When Sennacherib prepared to destroy the two and one-half tribes and overthrow Zion (chap. 63), Hezekiah prayed to God and reminded Him that Sennacherib would be boastful after he had destroyed Zion. Because of Hezekiah's righteousness, God heard his prayer and sent Ramiel to destroy the enemy. In contrast (chaps. 64-65), Manasseh practiced all sorts of cultic abominations. In response, God decided that Zion would be uprooted and two and one-half tribes taken captive.[61] Despite his prayer, Manasseh was not forgiven; because he was not worthy, his home was the fire.[62] We will see later how the author of 2 Baruch has used the contrast between the times of Hezekiah and Manasseh as a model for the situation of his own time.[63]

Baruch's response to the interpretation of the vision is a doxology (chap. 75). His earlier frustration over God's incomprehensibility is replaced by praise of God's incomprehensible goodness and His infinite mercy (75:1-6).[64] However, praise of God is not Baruch's final word. He

---

[60]By describing the rebuilding of the Temple, the author moves from the time in which the book is set to his own time period. Interestingly, he does not discuss the destruction of the Second Temple but proceeds immediately from the building of that Temple to the final times.

[61]Here the interpretation follows the biblical text. See 2 Kgs 21:10-18.

[62]This is one variation of legendary traditions about Manasseh which are recorded in Josephus (*Ant.* 10:177-183 [3,1-2]) and in a number of rabbinic texts (e.g., *m. Sanh.* 10:2; *Num. Rab.* 14:1; *Abot. R. Nat.* 36). The conflicting accounts within the Scriptures regarding Manasseh's ultimate destiny (2 Kgs 21:1-18; 2 Chr 33:1-23) probably were responsible for these legendary developments. For a discussion of the alternative forms of the legend, see Bogaert, *Apocalypse*, 1. 296-304.

[63]See below, Excursus A.

[64]Cf. Rom 11:33-36. Paul's lengthy theodicy argument (chaps. 9-11) culminates in praise, as does the vindication of God as just and powerful in 2 Baruch.

returns to the covenantal imagery of his conversations with God in Blocks 2, 4, and 5 in order to deliver a rhetorical exhortation to his community:

> If we who exist *know* from where we have come and *submit* to Him who brought us out of Egypt, we will come again and remember those things which have passed and rejoice regarding that which has been. But if we do not *know* from where we have come and recognize not the principate of Him who brought us out of Egypt, we will come again and seek those things which have been now, and be grieved with pain because of that which has happened. (75:7-8)

Here Baruch answers two of his initial questions (cf. 1B—3:4-9) by affirming that Israel has a future and that the Mosaic covenant retains its efficacy. He promises his community that knowledge of their covenantal past and continued submission to the God of the covenant will lead to rejoicing.[65] Through knowledge and submission, consolation is possible even in the present time. As we will see, this theological understanding is applied to the very practical questions of Baruch's community.

Summary

In Blocks 5-6, a consoled Baruch acknowledges and joyfully affirms God's vindication of Himself as just and powerful. The integration of motifs from earlier discussions regarding God's power and His justice provides the framework for God's final comments and for Baruch's expressions of consolation.

The basis of Baruch's consolation is his new perspective on the final times. Secure in his knowledge that God's justice and power will be manifest on an eschatological level, Baruch is able to affirm that God is just and powerful even in the present times.

In addition to expressing his own consolation, Baruch continues to be concerned about the *few* Jews who have remained loyal to their covenantal heritage. He intercedes for these people, and confidently asserts that the Torah is the basis of their continued existence in this world. He exhorts them to submit to the Torah and to the God of the covenant. In so doing, he assures them that God's covenant relationship with them has

---

[65]This is the converse of 12:3. Babylon is warned that her rejoicing will not continue indefinitely; Baruch's community are assured that eventually they will rejoice.

not been nullified. God's revelations to them about their future and their past make consolation possible even in the present troubled times.

THE SURVIVAL OF THE JEWISH COMMUNITY

Introduction

The second primary issue in 2 Baruch is the survival of the faithful Jewish community in the aftermath of the destruction. There are two facets to the development of this issue. (1) The loss of the land by destruction and dispersion calls into question the ability and willingness of God to keep the promises which He made to Abraham and to Moses.[66] (2) The impending death of Baruch, the last of the pre-destruction leaders, raises the practical question of whether Israel can even survive without his leadership. The question of the efficacy of God's promises about the land is treated explicitly in Baruch's initial questions (1B—3:4-9) and in his final speech to his people (77:2-10). It is treated implicitly through various geographical references in the book. The question of ongoing leadership is developed in the context of Baruch's encounters with his people. In response to their questions to him, Baruch begins the process of convincing them that his death will not mean the end of the community. Leadership under the Torah will not be lacking to Israel as long as time endures.

The following paragraphs trace the development of each facet of this issue. The first part of the analysis considers the existential question raised by the loss of the land that God promised to Abraham's descendants forever. The second part attempts to show how the practical question of ongoing leadership is raised and resolved in the context of Baruch's encounters with his people.

The Loss of the Land

Block 1 (Chapters 1-5)

Baruch's questions to God in their initial conversation (3:5-9) empha-

---

[66]The phrase "loss of land" refers to a complex of crises confronting the Jewish community in the time in which 2 Baruch was composed: the continued dispersion of Jews from the land; the devastation of the land of Judah by the Roman troops and the appropriation by them of some private property; and the destruction of the Temple and the land on which it stood. See E. M. Smallwood, *The Jews Under Roman Rule* (Leiden: E. J. Brill, 1976) 330-55.

size that the loss of the land poses a threat to the survival of the community:

> If you *destroy our city* and *deliver up Your land* to those that hate us, how will the name of Israel be remembered? . . . or how shall anyone speak Your praises? . . . or to whom shall that which is in Your Torah be explained? . . . and where is everything that You said to Moses about us? (3:5-9)

The destruction of the city and the delivering of the land to the enemy call into question the promises God made to Abraham and Moses. If those promises fail, then Israel has no future whatsoever.

Blocks 2-6 (Chapters 6-76)

The crisis caused by the loss of the land that God promised to Abraham is indirectly described and resolved in Blocks 2-6. The geographical location of the encounters between Baruch and his people highlights the crisis caused by the loss of Jerusalem, the symbolic center of the land promised to Abraham.[67] Baruch's community never assembles in Jerusalem. Throughout the book, Baruch receives revelation in the Temple area and then leaves the city to meet the people in the Kidron valley or in an unspecified location. He alone has access to the desolate city and, now that his death is approaching, even this tenuous connection to Jerusalem will be severed.

The resolution of this crisis is expressed through a typology between Baruch and Abraham, which also is evident in a number of other places (see Excursus A). The typology first occurs in the narrative of the destruction of Jerusalem (6:1-8:2). As the Babylonian army surrounds the city, Baruch leaves the people and goes to an oak tree (*blwt³*) (6:1). As he stands by the tree grieving over the impending destruction, he is suddenly lifted over the city and allowed to watch the angels set the walls on fire. This sets the stage for the seizure of God's city by the enemy. Baruch's experience by the oak tree (6:1-8:2) is the converse of Abraham's

---

[67] The relationship between the covenant with Abraham and the possession of the land is essential to the Abraham tradition in Genesis. See W. D. Davies, *The Gospel and the Land: Early Christianity and Jewish Territorial Doctrine* (Berkeley: University of California Press, 1974) 15-24. Cf. Helmut Köster, "*Topos*" *TDNT* 8 (1972) 195-99.

experience at a terebinth or oak tree.[68] According to Genesis 12:6-7, the tree was the scene of God's promise to Abraham that his descendants would in inherit the land:

> Abram passed through the country to . . . the terebinth tree
> at Moreh. . . . There the Lord appeared to Abram and said, I
> will give this land to your descendants. (12:6-7)[69]

Abraham received the promise that his descendants would inherit the land as he stood by the tree: Baruch witnesses the loss of that land to Babylon as he stands by the same kind of tree. By establishing the typology between Baruch and Abraham at this point, the author reiterates the seriousness of the question being addressed: how can God vindicate His decision to allow the enemy to seize the land promised to Abraham's descendants forever?

The answer to this question is expressed through another implicit comparison between Baruch and Abraham, this time in Block 5. After Baruch has assured the people that, despite his death, leadership under the Torah will not be lacking to the faithful community, he tells them ". . . behold, I go to Hebron because the Mighty One has sent me there" (47:1). The announced departure to Hebron is peculiar because Baruch never goes there, and indeed it never is mentioned again.[70] However, when the reference to Hebron is analyzed in its context, as the conclusion of a conversation which begins with Baruch's announcement of his impending death, the peculiarity is explained. The author is establishing a rela-

---

[68]Based on the process of retroversion, it is possible to argue that the Syriac term "oak" (*blwt²*) probably identifies the same kind of tree described in Gen 12:6-7 as "terebinth" (*²lwn*). The meaning of the Hebrew term *²lwn* is ambiguous. In the LXX it is translated *drys,* which means "oak." This meaning is carried over into the Peshitta version of Genesis, where *drys* (= Hebrew *²lwn*) is translated as *blwt².* Thus, the term used in 2 Baruch 6:1-2 to describe the tree where Baruch stood is the same term used in the Peshitta to describe the tree where Abraham stood (Gen 12:6-7). Moreover, the Syriac term accurately reflects the Greek translation of the Hebrew word *²lwn* as it appears in Gen 12:6-7.

[69]This promise is repeated throughout the Abraham story. Cf. Gen 13:14-18; chap. 15; chap. 18.

[70]Charles (*APOT,* 2. 504, n.7) agrees that the reference to Hebron is problematic. He suggests that the text is corrupt. Bogaert (*Apocalypse,* 2.84) simply notes that Hebron was the traditional burial place of the patriarchs and suggests that Baruch went there to die.

tionship between the deaths of Baruch and Abraham in order to resolve the questions raised by the loss of the land in Baruch's time. The key to this relationship is the scriptural account of the burial of Abraham.

According to Genesis 23 and 25:1-11, Sarah and Abraham both died before the promise of land was fulfilled. When Sarah died, Abraham purchased land for her burial from the Hittites who ruled Hebron. Later, Abraham also was buried there. Abraham never witnessed the fulfillment of God's promise about the land. However, by purchasing the grave at Hebron, a little bit of that land became his.[71] The burial of Sarah and Abraham at Hebron was a proleptic fulfillment of the promise that their descendants would inherit that land. Baruch witnesses the loss of the land inherited by Abraham's descendants to Babylon. The juxtaposition of the announcement of his death and of his departure to Hebron indicates his conviction that, despite appearances to the contrary, God's promise to Abraham has not been nullified. We do not know whether the reference to Hebron is intended only as a literary allusion or whether Baruch believes that he will die there. Nonetheless, the point remains—the faith of Abraham is matched by the confidence of Baruch.

Block 7 (Chapter 77)

A testamentary format provides the context for Baruch's final speech (see Excursus B). Just previously (chap. 76), he has learned that he will be taken from the earth. However, before that occurs, he returns to the people and, speaking with the authority of Moses, he delivers a final speech to them (77:2-10). Exile from the land and return to it are the primary themes in this speech:

> Hear you children of Israel, behold how many of you remain of the twelve tribes . . . to you and your fathers God gave a Torah more excellent than that of all nations. And because your brothers transgressed the commandments of the Most High, He brought vengeance on you and on them. And He spared not the former and the latter also He gave into captivity. But behold you are here with me. If therefore you direct your ways properly, you will not depart as did your brothers, but they will come to you. (77:2-6)

This message, delivered to people who have just witnessed the fall of their

---

[71]G. von Rad, Genesis (Philadelphia: Westminster Press, 1972) 250.

land to the enemy, is similar to that delivered by Moses to their ancestors prior to their initial entrance into the land. Moses said:

> When you have children and grandchildren and grow old in the land, if you then fall into the degrading practice of making any kind of carved figure, doing what is wrong in the eyes of the Lord your God and provoking him to anger, I summon heaven and earth to witness against you this day: you will soon vanish from the land which you are to occupy after crossing the Jordan. You will not live long in it; you will be swept away. The Lord will disperse you among the nations ... but if from there you seek the Lord your God, you will find Him, if indeed you search with all your heart and soul. When you are in distress and all these things come upon you, you will in days to come turn back to the Lord your God and obey Him. The Lord your God is a merciful god; He will never fail you nor destroy you, nor will He forget the covenant guaranteed by oath with your forefathers. (Deut 4:25-31)

Baruch, like Moses before him, emphasizes that the loss of land is not God's final word to His people. Despite the people's sin, God will forgive them and will bring back the exiles to land promised to Abraham's descendants forever.

This sense of forgiveness and covenantal fidelity is emphasized further in Baruch's subsequent characterization of God: "For He is merciful whom you serve and He is gracious in whom you hope, and He is true, so that He will do good and not evil" (77:7). This description echoes God's self-characterization in Exodus 34: "Yahweh, the Lord, a God merciful and gracious, long-suffering, ever constant and true" (Exodus 34:6).[72] These words, spoken by God to Moses on Mt. Sinai, characterize the God who has decided to forgive His people for their apostasy with the golden calf (Exodus 32:15-35) and to restore them to a covenant relationship with Him (Exodus 34:6-10ff.). Through his use of this terminology, Baruch reminds his community of God's loyalty to His covenantal commitment. If the people direct their ways properly, they will be forgiven and the exiles will return home to the land.[73]

---

[72] Previously (see above, pp. 56-57), I used the reference to "long-suffering" in Exod 34:6 as an example of the way in which the author of 2 Baruch deviates from the scriptural connotations of the term. Here the author uses the text to reiterate the scriptural emphasis on God's attitude of forgiveness toward His people.

[73] Given the eschatological tenor of 2 Baruch, it is likely that the

Summary

The existential question precipitated by the loss of the land is resolved by a vindication of God's loyalty to the covenant He made with Abraham and Moses. In various implicit and explicit ways, the people are assured that, despite appearances to the contrary, God has not defaulted on His promises to them. The covenant with Abraham and Moses remains efficacious even in the troubled present times.

Leadership Under the Torah

In Blocks 4, 5, and 7, the issue of the survival of the Jewish community is developed in terms of the ongoing leadership of that community. Baruch's speeches to his people and their conversations with him provide the format in which this theme is discussed.

Block 4 (Chapters 31-44)

Baruch first encounters his people after the destruction when he goes to them and tells them to assemble the elders in the Kidron valley (31:1-2). Baruch's instruction to the elders has a twofold purpose: to warn them that the present devastation is a harbinger of worse tribulations in the final times; and to assure them, nonetheless, that the Torah will protect the faithful community in these final turbulent times:

> Hear O Israel and I will speak to you, and give ear O seed of Jacob and I will instruct you . . . the days come when everything will become the prey of corruption . . . but if you prepare your hearts to sow in them the fruits of the Torah, it will protect you *in that time* (*bhw zbn*ʾ) when the Mighty One will shake creation. (31:3, 5; 32:1)

The content of Baruch's instruction draws on the revelations he received in Blocks 2 and 3. His warning about the shaking of creation *in that time* is based on the description of the final times given to him by God in the preceding Block of material (3C—chaps. 22-30). His assertion that a proper attitude toward the Torah will protect the people indicates that God's defense of His justice in Block 2 (2D—chaps. 13-20) has con-

---

author here is referring to the eschaton, rather than to the historical return of the exiles after the dispersion of 587 B.C.E.

vinced Baruch that obedience to the Torah is efficacious. In this way, Baruch makes public relevant points from the revelations communicated to him privately by God.

In this particular encounter, the elders do not respond to Baruch's speech to them. However, as Baruch departs from the valley, the people's reaction brings to the foreground the question of ongoing leadership:

> They [the people] lifted their voices and lamented and said: why are you departing from us Baruch and abandoning us like a father who abandons his orphan children and departs from them? . . . if you abandon us, it would be better for all of us to die before you, than that you should withdraw from us. (32:8-9; 33:3)

Baruch's community regards him as their "father" and their sole surviving leader. They perceive any sign of his departure from them as a threat to their very existence.

Baruch responds by assuring the people (chap. 34) that, far from abandoning them, he is going to the Temple ruins to seek further enlightenment about them and Zion. Then he leaves them. This conversation foreshadows Baruch's next encounter with his people. There he and they will have to deal with his permanent departure from them.

Block 5 (Chapters 44-52)

Block 5 begins as Baruch summons a group of persons from his community[74] and deals explicitly with the question of ongoing leadership under the Torah (44:1). It becomes clear that these persons are Baruch's designated successors. Baruch begins and concludes his speech to them by juxtaposing two themes: the transition in the leadership of the community from himself to them; and their responsibility to instruct the people in the Torah in order to insure the survival of the community. He states:

> Behold I go to my fathers according to the way of all the

---

[74]This group is identified only as Baruch's oldest son, seven elders, and perhaps "Gedaliah my friend" (44:1). The text is corrupt. Charles (*APOT*, 2. 502) translates it as "Gedaliahs my friends," while Bogaert (*Apocalypse*, 2. 78-79) emends it to "Gedaliah my friend." Interestingly, the name "Gedaliah" is not included when Baruch's hearers respond to his words (45:1).

> earth. Do not withdraw from the way of the Torah, but
> preserve and admonish the people who remain. (44:2-3)

> Therefore, as far as you are able, instruct the people, for that
> work is ours. For if you teach them, you will make them
> alive. (chap. 45)[75]

Previously, Baruch instructed Israel (4B—31:3); now he exhorts his successors to instruct the people. He has transferred the mantle of leadership
from himself to them.

In the remainder of this speech, Baruch shares with his successors
part of the revelation he has received. In particular, he emphasizes that
God is just and will allow the righteous to participate in the future world
and time (44:5-15). The various expressions that Baruch uses to acknowledge God's justice in this speech indicate that he has attained consolation
in regard to his earlier questions. Previously, he argued that the destruction should have been averted because of the works of those who served
(plḥw) the good (14:7). Here he repeats the verb "serve" to affirm "you
see that He whom we serve (plḥyn) is just" (44:4). Previously, he expressed
his despair over God's apparent lack of justice by asking "who will search
out (mᶜqb) the depths of Your ways?" (14:8). Here he acknowledges that
". . . The judgment of the Mighty One will be known, and His ways, which
cannot be sought out (mtᶜqbn) are right" (44:6).

The verses that immediately precede and follow Baruch's acknowledgment of God's justice (44:3,7) connect his general statements to the
specific situation of his community. Terminology from Block 4 is used to
exhort Baruch's hearers to remain loyal to the Torah in confidence of an
eschatological reward.[76] Baruch states:

> . . . do not withdraw from the way of the Torah and guard and
> admonish the people who remain so that they will not with-
> draw from the commands of the Mighty One. (44:3)

---

[75]Cf. Deut 30:15-20. There the people are told that to obey the
covenant is to choose life. Here Baruch's successors are told that by
teaching the people that covenant they will enable them to continue making the choice of life.

[76]The emphasis on the Torah and its interpretation also characterized later rabbinic Judaism. See Moore, *Judaism*, 1. 235-80, 308-22.

> . . . if you endure and remain firm in His fear, and do not
> forget the Torah, the times will change for you for the *good*
> and you will see the consolation of Zion. (44:7)

The term "withdraw" appeared in Block 4 (42:3-4) as a description of Jews who forfeited the covenant status and therefore forfeited any participation in the future time. Here the exhortation "do not withdraw" distinguishes Baruch's community from those Jews and reiterates the importance of maintaining the covenant status through a proper attitude toward the Torah. The promise that loyalty to the Torah will lead to "good" echoes God's statement in Block 4 that "to those with faith there will be the good"[77] at the final times (42:2). In these ways, Baruch applies what he has learned about God's justice in Blocks 2 and 4 to the needs of the community which soon he will leave behind.

The remainder of Baruch's speech consists of an elaboration of the promised "good" in terms of participation in the new world and the new time. Baruch's description of this eschatological realm, previously described to him by God,[78] gives impetus to obey the Torah in this world. The characteristics of those persons privileged to inherit the new world and time (44:14) are elaborations of the credentials presented by Baruch in his second prayer (4F—chap. 38). Baruch's attitude toward the Torah and wisdom[79] made him a worthy recipient of God's revelation; that same attitude makes his community worthy recipients of the new world and time.

After Baruch has concluded his speech, his hearers react immediately to his message. Their anger and panic indicate that Baruch's promise about the future world is not sufficient to enable them to cope without him in the present world:

---

[77] The use of the term "good" reiterates the covenantal overtones of this segment. See above, n. 20.

[78] The description occurs primarily in Blocks 2 (2D—15:7-8) and 4 (4G—42:4-43:3). There are a few references to motifs discussed in Block 3—e.g., the corruptible/incorruptible distinction (44:8-9; cf. 3B—21:19).

[79] The practice of juxtaposing Torah and wisdom in this way was rather widespread in this time. For discussions of the origin and evolution of this development, see: Martin Hengel, *Judaism and Hellenism* (Philadelphia: Fortress Press, 1974) 1. 153-75; Gerhard von Rad, *Wisdom in Israel* (Nashville: Abingdon Press, 1972) 240-62.

> Has God humiliated us (*mkkn*) to such a degree that He would
> take you from us so quickly (*bᶜgᵭ*)? And truly we will be in
> darkness and there will be no light to the people who are
> left. For where shall we seek the Torah or who will distin-
> guish for us between life and death? (46:1-3)

The great gap between Baruch's anticipation of the future world and his
hearers' despair over life without him in this world is evident in this
reworking of a previous statement. When referring to the present world
in contrast to the future world, Baruch states ". . . that which (now)
prospers shall (then) fall quickly (*bᶜgᵭ*) and be humiliated (*mtmkkᵭ*)" (44:10).
Baruch's hearers adapt the phrase "humiliated quickly" to express their
dismay over the prospect of life in this world without Baruch: ". . . has
God humiliated us so as to take you from us so quickly?" (46:1). Clearly,
Baruch's portrayal of the final times has not been sufficient to enable his
hearers to cope with the present time.

Baruch responds to this despair by expanding his earlier statements
about leadership under the Torah. Speaking to the whole community,[80] he
asserts:

> The throne of the Mighty One I cannot resist;[81] nevertheless,
> there shall not be lacking to Israel a wise man nor a son of
> the Torah to the race of Jacob.[82] But only prepare your
> hearts to obey the Torah and submit to those who in fear are
> wise and understanding, and prepare your souls not to with-
> draw from them. For if you do these things, good tidings will
> come to you and you will not fall into the torment of which I
> previously testified to you. (46:4-6)

This segment began as Baruch transferred the leadership of the community from himself to his successors. It concludes as he promises that
leadership under the Torah will never be lacking to the faithful community.

_____

[80]The identity of the community as Baruch's addressee is implied.
See above, chap. 2, n. 18.

[81]Cf. 3:1-3 (1B), where Baruch states: ". . . take my spirit that I
might go to my fathers . . . I can not *resist* You and my soul can not
endure the evils of my mother." There Baruch spoke in despair. Here he
speaks in confidence that his community will survive his death.

[82]The identity of the "wise man" and "son of the Torah" is never
described. It is uncertain whether either term is used in any kind of
technical sense.

Block 7 (Chapter 77)

In Block 7 (chap. 77), Baruch gathers all the people, from the greatest to the least (77:1).[83] Unlike his earlier speeches to representatives of
his community, Baruch's final speech deals only with the covenant relationship between God and Israel. The question of leadership under the
Torah is not addressed.

The leadership issue emerges, however, in the people's response to
Baruch's words. For the first time, there is no panic in their reaction.
They state their intention to remember the *good* which God has done as
best they can,[84] and they ask Baruch to write to the brothers in Babylon
in order to strengthen them before he dies (77:11-12). The reasons which
they give for their request provide the foil which Baruch will use to make
his final statement to them:

> For the shepherds of Israel have perished and the lamps which
> gave light are extinguished, and the fountains have withheld
> their stream from which we used to drink. And we are aban-
> doned in the darkness and without the counsel of shepherds,[85]
> and in the thirst of the wilderness. (77:13-14)

In response, Baruch once more addresses the question of whether
his community (Israel) will survive:

> Shepherds and lamps and fountains come from the Torah: and
> although we depart the Torah remains. If therefore you hold
> to the Torah and are eager for wisdom, a lamp will not be
> wanting and a shepherd will not fail and a fountain will not
> dry up. (77:15-16)

The perpetuity of the Torah guarantees to the faithful community the

---

[83]The statement that Baruch gathered all his people "from the
greatest to the least" (77:1) has a definite Jeremianic flavor. Several
times, Jeremiah uses the phrase "the least to the greatest" either to
describe the people's violation of the covenant or to emphasize God's
never-ending covenant fidelity (6:13; 8:10; 31:34; 42:1,8).

[84]This again is covenantal imagery. Cf. above, n. 20.

[85]The phrase is corrupt. I have followed the emendation of F.
Zimmerman, "Textual Observations on the Apocalypse of Baruch," *JTS* 40
(1939) 151-56.

leadership and other resources it will need for its survival. Israel does have a future, even in the present troubled times.

2 Baruch concludes as Baruch leaves the people (77:18-26) to write the letter requested by them and to write an identical letter to the nine and one-half tribes. He sits by an oak tree, composes the letters, and dispatches them to their recipients by three men and by an eagle.

The reference to Baruch's activity under the oak tree integrates both formats of the survival issue by situating Baruch's last task as leader in a geographical location important to the loss of land motif. Previously (2A—chap. 6) Baruch observed the loss of the land promised to Abraham's descendants as he stood by an oak tree. Now, after he has learned that God remains faithful to His people despite the loss of land and that He guarantees perpetuity of leadership under the Torah, Baruch returns to an oak to transmit this message to all Jews everywhere.

Summary

In Blocks 4, 5, and 7, Baruch's grieving community raises questions which compel Baruch to vindicate God's promise that there will continue to be descendants of Abraham to whom the promises apply. He does this by applying the revelations he has received to the practical question of ongoing leadership of the community. He assures His people that they do have a future in this world; leaders will continue to arise for the community faithful to the Torah as long as time endures. In addition , they have an eschatological future; submission to the Torah and its teachers in this world will lead to participation in the future world and time. By transferring leadership from himself to his successors, Baruch enables the community to take its first step into its future without him. Through his words and actions, he conveys to the people his conviction that God's covenant relationship with them has not been nullified.

CONCLUSION

This examination of the issues of 2 Baruch has revealed how the author uses the story as the vehicle through which he raises and resolves the issues with which he is concerned. The blocks of material through which the story unfolds are related to one another on the basis of content, terminology, and structure.

Both of the primary issues with which the author is concerned are parts of an argument about theodicy. Baruch's questions and those of his people are variations on one major question: Has God nullified His covenantal relationship with the faithful Jews who constitute "Israel"? The answer to this question is a resounding "No!" Through his conversations with God, Baruch learns that the Mosaic covenant has not lost its efficacy. God vindicates Himself as just and powerful in regard to the present situation by giving Baruch a preview of the eschatological manifestation of His justice and power. As a result, Baruch is able to promise his community that submission to the Torah and faith in the God of the covenant are the key to consolation in this world and to participation in the future world and time. Through their conversations with Baruch, his community learns that, despite appearances to the contrary, God's promises to Abraham have not been nullified. Baruch vindicates these promises through his words and his actions. By announcing that he is going to Hebron and by promising that the exiles will return, Baruch assures the people that the loss of the land promised to Abraham's descendants is not God's last word to them. They will be forgiven and consoled. By promising that leadership under the Torah will never be lacking to the faithful community, Baruch assures the people that there will continue to be descendants of Abraham to whom the promises will apply.

In summary, throughout the story told in 2 Baruch, the argument about theodicy is developed from the perspective of the continued efficacy of God's covenant relationship with His people. It is resolved in two ways. The promise of the eschatological future affirms the efficacy of the Mosaic covenant in the present times. The promise that the community will survive in the present times and will have a better future affirms the covenant God made with Abraham about his descendants and the land.[86]

EVALUATION OF PREVIOUS RESEARCH

The holistic understanding of 2 Baruch which has emerged from the literary analysis of the book offers a helpful perspective from which to evaluate the contributions of other scholars to research on the document.

---

[86]This does not mean that the figure of Moses is mentioned only in the context of God's discussions about His justice or that Abraham appears only in discussions about the future of the community. On the contrary, when he addresses the issue of God's justice, Baruch speaks as if he were Abraham (2D—chap. 14; see Excursus A), and when he assures the community for the final time that they have a future, he speaks as if he were Moses (7B—77:2-10; see Excursus B). Thus, both biblical figures and covenants overlap with each other throughout the book.

These scholars include: R. H. Charles, P.-M. Bogaert, W. Harnisch, A. C. B. Kolenkow, and A. Thompson.

By translating the text of 2 Baruch into English, R. H. Charles has made an invaluable contribution to the study of the document. However, because of his determination to isolate the sources of which the document is composed, he has not observed that there is an integrity to the book which supersedes the presence of various sources and traditions. The author of 2 Baruch certainly has used a variety of different, and some-times conflicting, traditions.[87] However, as we have seen, he has inte-grated these traditions into a unified, coherent whole.

P.-M. Bogaert has correctly ascertained that 2 Baruch is a unified composition which can be divided into sections. In the notes to Chapter II, I have already appraised the boundaries he suggests for each section and the criteria he has used to determine them.[88] However, the primary problem with his approach to the literary unity of the book is not that he has misplaced the boundaries of some of the literary sections. Rather, his approach is problematic because, in segmenting the text into sections, he has lost sight of the whole which is greater than the simple sum of its parts.[89] He has not addressed the question of how the individual parts are related to one other and integrated with one other to form the literary whole.

Bogaert's contributions to research on 2 Baruch include isolating a number of the central themes in the book.[90] However, because he ana-lyzes these themes in isolation from their context within the unfolding of the story, Bogaert does not always recognize the questions which are being addressed and resolved. His topical study of the "great themes" illustrates this point.

Bogaert begins his examination of the "great themes" in 2 Baruch[91] by observing quite accurately that the goal of 2 Baruch is to reveal the

---

[87]For example, the author clearly has used different traditions about the tribulations of the end-times in 25:1-29:1; 48:29-41; and chaps. 70-71. Also, as Charles has observed (*APOT*, 2. 474-76), the author is not at all consistent regarding the relationship of the Messiah to the end-times (e.g., 29:2-30:2; chaps. 39-40; chaps. 72-74). However, as this analysis has shown, the author has incorporated all of these different traditions into a unified literary whole.

[88]See above, Chapter II, notes 7, 10, 14, 19, 23, 25.

[89]See the discussion in Bogaert, *Apocalypse*, 1. 57-67.

[90]Ibid., 1. 381-444.

[91]Ibid., 386-92.

meaning of the catastrophic events in Jerusalem and to give hope in the
efficacy of observance of the Torah at the moment when sacrifices
become impossible or very difficult.[92] However, he does not ask how the
questions of meaning are formulated throughout the book or in what
context the emphasis on the observance of the Torah is developed.
Instead, he subdivides the topic into two parts: the sense of suffering and
hope; and the Temple and the Torah. In the first part, Bogaert concludes
that in 2 Baruch the doctrine of suffering is based on the expiatory value
of suffering in this world and on the promise of consolation in the future
world. He compares this view to that of certain rabbis and of 4 Ezra. In
the second part, he observes that the Temple is more important in
2 Baruch than in 4 Ezra and that the replacement of the Temple by the
Torah was necessary for the survival of Judaism after 70 C.E. This concludes his study of the "great themes" of 2 Baruch.

Bogaert has correctly suggested that "suffering" and "Torah" are
important motifs in 2 Baruch. However, because he has investigated them
only by identifying where the terms occur and then making generalizations on the basis of this identification, he has not been able to refine the
significance of each motif in terms of the question it is being used to
address. My method has revealed that the question of meaning addressed
by both of these motifs is that of God's covenant fidelity: Has the covenant with Abraham and Moses been nullified? This question is raised
repeatedly and in different ways throughout the text. Likewise, the
answer to it is repeated systematically until it is accepted by both Baruch
and his community. The significance of the motifs of "suffering" and
"Torah" is based on their presence within the process of raising and
resolving this question.

Given the self-imposed limitations of his study, W. Harnisch perhaps has made the most significant contribution to the understanding of
one of the primary issues of 2 Baruch. His analysis of the eschatological
dimensions of the vindication of God's justice is perceptive and helpful.[93]
However, E. Breech's criticism of Harnisch's approach to 4 Ezra applies
also to 2 Baruch:

---

[92]Bogaert clearly assumes that the author of 2 Baruch accepted the
validity of the Temple cult prior to the destruction. His statement
regarding the goal of the book is somewhat unexpected in view of his
thesis that 2 Baruch was written for Jews in the diaspora (*Apocalypse*, 1.
335).
[93]Harnisch, *Verhängnis*. The main points of his analysis of 2 Baruch
have been summarized in the notes to this chapter. See above, notes 5,
12, 14, 35, 50, 54.

Unfortunately, Harnisch does not support this assertion [regarding the function of Ezra] by literary analysis. He
simply states this view as a basic "key" which unlocks the box
containing the author's theology of history. Harnisch's view
thus persists in treating the form of 4 Ezra as a container for
ideas. Structure and meaning remain relatively separate.[94]

Because he treats 2 Baruch as a "container for ideas," Harnisch does not
take into account the relationship between structure and meaning
throughout the book. Thus, although he summarizes accurately the eschatological resolution of one of the primary issues, he is not fully cognizant
of the questions to which the resolution is a response. He does not differentiate between the questions raised regarding God's justice and those
raised regarding His power. He also does not observe that the center
around which the discussion on God's justice revolves is the method used
by God in one particular situation to exercise His justice to Israel and the
nations. Because he assumes that the fulcrum is the free will of man, he
does not note the manner in which God's statements about freedom of
choice function to introduce a discussion about the righteous and the
wicked within Israel. Finally, because he has concentrated solely on the
conversations between God and Baruch, Harnisch has not dealt with the
dimensions of theodicy implied by the apparent negation of God's promise
regarding the possession of the land.

These criticisms of Harnisch's approach do not negate the value of
his research. However, they do illustrate the problems which arise when
the issues of 2 Baruch are examined as theological propositions, rather
than as parts of an unfolding story.

A. C. B. Kolenkow has brought to the foreground the visionary
material of 2 Baruch (4E, G—chaps. 36-40; 6B, E—chaps. 53, 55-76).[95] By
isolating this material and examining it in conjunction with relevant
segments of 4 Ezra, she attempts to show that the visionary material in
2 Baruch is dependent on 4 Ezra 4, 11-13. She concludes that at least
some of the visionary material in 2 Baruch was composed to correct the
view of the end-times in 4 Ezra. The support Kolenkow adduces for her
thesis is weak.[96] However, the primary shortcoming of the thesis itself is

---

[94]Earl Breech, "These Fragments I have Shored against My Ruins:
The Form and Function of 4 Ezra," *JBL* 92 (1973) 269.

[95]A. C. B. Kolenkow, *An Introduction to 2 Baruch 53-74: Structure
and Substance* (Harvard Ph.D., 1971).

[96]Ibid., 1-31. Kolenkow probably is correct when she states the vis-

the presuppositon that it is possible to determine the intention of a portion of 2 Baruch without reference to its context within the structure of
the entire book. The question of the relationship of traditions used in
2 Baruch to those used in 4 Ezra is secondary to that of their function
within 2 Baruch. The analysis of 2 Baruch has revealed that the cedar/
vine vision functions as an example of the final manifestation of God's
justice against the nation presently oppressing His people. The cloud/
waters vision enables the author to apply God's general plan for mankind
to the details of Israel's history. The significance of these visions is their
position within the unfolding of the story which is being told throughout
2 Baruch. The isolation of these texts from the rest of the document does
not do justice to their setting and function within the literary whole.

        A. Thompson has attempted to analyze the arguments about theod-
icy in 4 Ezra and 2 Baruch side-by-side. Since Thompson's stated goal is
to prove that the form and structure of 4 Ezra is the key to its meaning,[97] it would seem logical that he would approach 2 Baruch from the
same methodological perspective. However, he does not do so. Instead,
he projects the form and structure of 4 Ezra onto 2 Baruch. As a result,
he argues that "the dominant trend of the book (2 Baruch) is that man is
quite capable of obeying God's commands, and therefore able to gain
future bliss by merit."[98] Because Thompson has projected the concerns of
4 Ezra onto 2 Baruch, he has neither identified nor addressed the questions which are raised and resolved in 2 Baruch. His research is helpful in
illustrating the problems which arise when the agenda of 4 Ezra is used as
a model for that of 2 Baruch.

        In summary, scholars have analyzed 2 Baruch from a variety of

----

ionary material in 4 Ezra and 2 Baruch reflects traditions recorded in
Daniel 7. However, her argument that 2 Baruch 53, 56-74 is directly
dependent on 4 Ezra 4, 11-13 is not convincing for a variety of reasons.
For example, in order to show that the Danielic traditions are transmitted
to 2 Baruch through 4 Ezra, she tries to connect the cloud/waters imagery
in 2 Baruch 53 to 4 Ezra 4:48-50. In the 4 Ezra reference, Ezra sees a
raincloud pass over and leave a few raindrops behind. The point of this
illustration is to show Ezra that the final times are approaching.
Kolenkow seems to assume that the author of 2 Baruch develops this illustration into a full-blown vision about a cloud which rained waters on the
earth (53:1b-11).
        [97] A. Thompson, *Responsibility for Evil in the Theodicy of 4 Ezra*
(SBLDS 29; Missoula: Scholars Press, 1977) 1-2.
        [98] Ibid., 133.

perspectives and, in the process, have made some important contributions to the understanding of the document. However, because they have not approached the document holistically, they have not grasped how the individual parts are part of a greater whole. Thus, their research suffers from a lack of completeness.

The literary analysis undertaken in Chapter II of the dissertation has revealed that the key to the structure of 2 Baruch is the story which is being told through the clustering and arrangement of the individual literary sub-units. The exposition of the primary issues of the book in this chapter has verified the results of that literary analysis. Moreoever, it has become apparent that the story is the vehicle through which the author raises and resolves the question of whether God has nullified His covenantal relationship with Israel. This question permeates the discussion on God's justice and power and the discussion on the survival of the faithful community. It is the controlling theme in the story which is being told through the clustering and arrangement of the various literary sub-units.

EXCURSUS A:

THE FIGURE OF ABRAHAM AND THE
STORY OF SODOM IN 2 BARUCH

The figure of Abraham and the story of Sodom play an important, although implicit, role in the defense of God's justice in 2 Baruch. By comparing the presence of these motifs in 2 Baruch with their Scriptural antecedents and with the *Martyrdom of Isaiah*, it is possible to assess more clearly their meaning and function in 2 Baruch.

Imagery from the Abraham tradition appears in several contexts in 2 Baruch. The biblical story of Abraham haggling with God over the imminent destruction of Sodom and Gomorrah (Genesis 18:16-33) is the model for Baruch's haggling with God after the destruction of Jerusalem (2D—chaps. 14-20). The traditional characterization of Abraham as a "man of faith"[99] is adapted as a description of the community loyal to Moses' heritage.

---

[99]The characterization of Abraham as a "man of faith" is based on Genesis 15:6: "And Abraham put his faith in the Lord and the Lord counted that faith as righteousness."

The first example of terminology common to the Abraham tradition and to 2 Baruch appears in Block 1 (1B—chap. 3). God's initial announcement to Baruch that Jerusalem will be destroyed because of the people's sins (chap. 1) is followed by Baruch's assertion that death is preferable to the sight of the punishment of his mother (3:1-3). The phrase used by Baruch to introduce his death-wish—"if I have found grace in Your eyes"—is the same as that used by Abraham to welcome the guests who are on their way to Sodom (Genesis 18:3).[100]

The parallel between Abraham and Baruch becomes explicit when Abraham's haggling with God prior to the destruction of Sodom (Genesis 18) is compared with Baruch's haggling with God after the destruction of Jerusalem (2D—chap. 14). In Genesis 18:16-33, Abraham argues with God about the number of righteous inhabitants necessary to avert the destruction of Sodom. God concurs with Abraham's premise that righteousness should be a deterrent to destruction; eventually, however, He does destroy Sodom because not even ten righteous men inhabit it. In 2 Baruch 14, Baruch uses Abraham's premise in order to argue that God's decision to destroy Jerusalem is incomprehensible:

> . . . what have they profited who had knowledge of You . . . and have not said to the dead: 'Give us life,' but have always feared you and have not left Your ways? And . . . they have been carried off and You have not had mercy on Zion because of them. And if others did evil, it was due to Zion, that on account of those who do good works, she should be forgiven and should not be overwhelmed on account of the works of those who worked unrighteousness. But who, O Lord, can comprehend Your judgment. (14:5-8)

From Baruch's perspective, the righteousness of some of its inhabitants should have deterred God from destroying Jerusalem. The sins of its other inhabitants should not have swayed His decision so decisively.

As the conversation continues (15:1-19:3), it becomes clear that

---

[100]This terminology is not unique to the Abraham tradition. In fact, Baruch's anguish in chap. 3 is similar to that of Moses in Numbers 11:15. There Moses asks that "if he has found favor in God's eyes" he not be made to bear the burden of the people alone. Thus the similarity in terminology between 2 Baruch 3:1-3 and Genesis 18:3 does not establish an Abraham/Baruch typology; it is merely the first example of terminology which appears both in the Abraham tradition and in 2 Baruch.

Baruch's argument is a foil used by God primarily to explicate the magnitude of the sins of Jerusalem's inhabitants. God deals only briefly with the righteous (15:7-8), choosing instead to concentrate on the non-righteous members of the Jewish community. The resulting distinction between the *many* Jews who have chosen the darkness of Adam and the *few* Jews who have remained loyal to Moses' heritage (chap. 18) makes it clear that the righteous are a definite minority within the Jewish community. Jerusalem, like Sodom before it, was an extremely sinful city.

The conversation between God and Baruch in Block 4 (4G—chaps. 41-43) explicates further the sins of the *many* "unworthy" Jews who have chosen the darkness of Adam. In response to Baruch's question "who will be *worthy* to live at that time?" (41:1), God states that those persons who have faith will receive good, and those who despise will receive the contrary. Then He declares that those Jews who have withdrawn from the covenant and thrown off the yoke of the Torah by assimilating to the ways of the nations will not participate in the future time (42:4). Thus, these are the Jews who "despise" and are not "worthy." The term "worthy" appears again in the interpretation of the cloud/waters vision. Here it refers to Manasseh, who was judged by God to be "unworthy" to live despite his repentance. The sins which prompted God to deliver such a verdict were primarily cultic abuses, including idolatry. Although there is insufficient evidence to make a definite assertion, the use of the term "worthy" in these two contexts makes reasonable the conjecture that Manasseh is a prototype of the *many* Jews mentioned in the conversation of Block 4.

On the surface, the similarities between the *many* Jews and Manasseh say nothing about a Jerusalem/Sodom typology. However, when this material is compared to the tradition which is recorded in the *Martyrdom of Isaiah,* it becomes clear that there are grounds on which to suggest that there indeed is a Jerusalem/Sodom typology at work in this part of 2 Baruch.

The *Martyrdom of Isaiah* is a Jewish legend which culminates in the death of Isaiah at the hands of King Manasseh.[101] According to the legend, the devil Beliar dwells in Manasseh's heart and motivates him to transform the Temple cult into the worship of Satan (2:1-6). Isaiah and other righteous men leave the city for the desert, "lamenting with great lamentation because of the going astray of Israel" (2:10). The false

---

[101]For an introduction to the book, see G. Nickelsburg, *Jewish Literature,* 142-45.

prophet Belchir-ra accuses Isaiah of prophesying the destruction of Jerusalem and of referring to the city as Sodom and its princes as Gomorrah
(3:6-10).[102] Because Beliar dwells in his heart, Manasseh believes Belchir-ra and has Isaiah killed (3:11-5:14).

Thus, there is a legend in which the figure of Manasseh is explicitly
connected to a typology between Jerusalem/Sodom. The typology is based
on the perception that the cult in Jerusalem is defiled. In addition, there
is a tradition about Manasseh recorded in 2 Baruch 64-65 in which his
cultic abuses are emphasized. Moreover, there is some evidence to suggest that he is portrayed as the prototype of the Jews who have forfeited
the covenantal status. This evidence, in conjunction with the typology
between Jerusalem/Sodom implied earlier in 2 Baruch (chaps. 14-19),
supports the hypothesis that 2 Baruch says implicitly what the *Martyrdom
of Isaiah* says openly: the cult in Jerusalem prior to the destruction was
defiled to such a degree that Jerusalem was no better than Sodom before
it.

The implications of the Jerusalem/Sodom typology for an understanding of Jewish religious life at the turn of the common era are important. As is well known, the community of Qumran withdrew into the
wilderness to escape what it perceived to be the satanic cult in Jerusalem. Similarities between Qumran literature and the *Martyrdom of Isaiah*
have motivated some scholars to associate that document with the Qumran community.[103] Regardless of the relationship of the *Martyrdom of
Isaiah* to Qumran, 2 Baruch clearly has no connection with that community. The existence of implicit or explicit typologies between Jerusalem
and Sodom in these different types of documents testifies to what must
have been significant and divergent dissatisfaction with the Jerusalem
cult in the years prior to the destruction of the Temple.[104]

The use of imagery from the Abraham tradition in defense of God's
justice is not limited to the story of his haggling with God about the
destruction of Sodom. The ascription of Abraham's faith to Baruch is
evident in Baruch's announcement to his people that he is departing to

---

[102]As Charles observes (*APOT*, 2. 161, n. 10), this prophecy was
made by the biblical Isaiah (Isa 1:10).

[103]D. Flusser, "The Apocryphal Book of Ascensio Isaiae and the
Dead Sea Sect," *IEJ* 3 (1953) 30-47. See also Nickelsburg, *Jewish
Literature,* 144-45.

[104]The *Apocalypse of Abraham* is another example of an Abrahamic
tradition in which the figure of Manasseh and the theme of cultic defilement appear. We will discuss this book further in Chapter V.

Hebron (47:1).[105] Moreover, "faith" is an important attribute of all the righteous in 2 Baruch. In response to Baruch's question about those persons worthy to live in the final times (4G—41:1) God declares that "to those with faith will be the good" (4G—42:2). Similarly, in his final prayer (6C—chap. 54), Baruch affirms that God gives the revelation necessary for consolation to those persons with "faith" (54:4-5), and he confidently asserts that the "faithful" will receive their reward (54:16).

EXCURSUS B:

MOSAIC TESTAMENTARY IMAGERY
IN 2 BARUCH

In addition to the material from the Abraham traditon, the author of 2 Baruch also has incorporated into his work motifs from the Mosaic testamentary tradition. The following examination of the Mosaic testamentary motifs in 2 Baruch deals with four questions: (1) What is a testament? (2) How do portions of 2 Baruch reflect a testamentary format? (3) What evidence is there of a Baruch/Moses typology in the testamentary material? (4) What is the function of the Mosaic testamentary material in 2 Baruch?

There is no consensus regarding the exact definition of the "testament" genre in the pseudepigraphal writings of the intertestamental period.[106] However, a number of books of this time period are called "testaments" and share a variety of common features.[107] The pattern followed throughout most of the *Testaments of the Twelve Patriarchs* illustrates the typical characteristics of a testament.[108] A dying patriarch summons his sons to his death-bed. He reviews some historical events from his life time, and delivers ethical exhortations and a prediction about the future. Then he dies and is buried at Hebron.[109]

---

[105]See above, pp. 77-78.

[106]M. de Jonge, "Review of E. von Nordheim, *Die Lehre der Alten,* 1," *JSJ* 12 (1981) 117.

[107]For an examination of the formal characteristics of testaments see E. von Nordheim, *Die Lehre der Alten,* 1 (Leiden: E. J. Brill, 1980). Particularly relevant in this context are pp. 10, 89-97.

[108]For a further discussion of the *Testaments of the Twelve Patriarchs,* see Nickelsburg, *Jewish Literature,* 232-41.

[109]At first glance, the reference to Hebron as the burial place of

The testamentary material in 2 Baruch follows this general format. Each of the encounters between Baruch and his people after the destruction illustrates one or more facets of the testamentary pattern. The encounter in Block 4 (4A-C—chaps. 31-34) establishes a "father/sons" relationship between Baruch and his people (32:9). This "father/sons" relationship reappears in the encounter in Block 5 (5A-D—chaps. 44-47). There the dying "father" delivers his testament to the "sons" who have been designated to succeed him as leaders of the people. The testamentary nature of Baruch's speech is evident in several ways. In addition to announcing his impending death (44:1-2), Baruch reminds his hearers of the past destruction (44:5) and predicts the eschatological destinies of the righteous and the wicked (44:7-15). His exhortation to remain loyal to the Torah and his predictions about the future are bracketed by the primary theme of the encounter: the transition in leadership from the "father" to the "sons" (5B—44:2-3; chap. 45). Baruch's final speech to his people (7B—77:2-10) also follows this format. In typical testamentary style, he reviews the history of the two dispersions, exhorts the people to direct their ways properly, and promises them that if they do so their dispersed brothers will return to them (77:2-10). The people indicate their acceptance of Baruch's impending departure by stating their intention to remember the good as best they can, and by asking Baruch to write to the brothers in Babylon in order to strengthen them before his death (7C—77:11-14). The revelations Baruch has received and shared throughout the book are his testament to his people: the letters he sends to the diaspora make that testament available to all Jews everywhere.

The relationship between the testamentary material in 2 Baruch and the Moses tradition becomes evident when the encounters between Baruch and his successors are compared to relevant portions of the *Testament of Moses*. This book is a re-writing of Deuteronomy 31:24-26.[110] Moses announces his impending death (1:15), commissions Joshua as his successor (1:7-11), commands Joshua to preserve the secret prophecies

_____

the patriarchs seems to establish a connection between the *Testaments* and Baruch's announcement (chap. 47) that he is going to Hebron. However, de Jonge (*The Testaments of the Twelve Patriarchs* [Assen: van Gorcum, 1975] second edition, 1975) suggests that the Hebron reference in the *Testaments* probably reflects the effort of a Christian redactor to impose a unity upon them. Thus, its value in relation to 2 Baruch is dubious.

[110]See Nickelsburg, *Jewish Literature*, 80-83. He discusses how the testamentary format in the *Testament of Moses* is based on Deut 31-34.

(1:16-18), and delivers extensive revelation about the history of Israel (chaps. 2-9). Joshua reacts with panic to this message, asking how Israel can possibly survive without Moses' leadership (chap. 11). In response, Moses assures him that God's covenant with Israel will never lose its efficacy (chap. 12).

It seems clear that the relationship of Baruch to his successors is modelled after that of Moses to Joshua. In his speech in Block 5 (5B), Baruch announces his impending death (44:2), transfers leadership from himself to his successors (44:2-3; chap. 45), exhorts them to preserve the people by teaching them the Torah (44:3; chap. 45), and delivers revelations about the immediate past (44:5) and the eschatological future (44:7-15). Baruch's successors react with panic to his message, asking how the faithful community can possibly survive with his leadership (5C—46:1-3). In response, Baruch assures them that leadership under the Torah will never be lacking for the faithful community (5C—44:4-6). The parallels between this encounter and the relevant portions of the *Testament of Moses* are one piece of evidence that there is a typology between Baruch and Moses in the testamentary material of 2 Baruch.

The final portion of the conversation between Baruch and Ramiel (6E—chaps. 75-76) provides the second piece of evidence of a Baruch/Moses typology in the testamentary material. Baruch responds to the interpretation of the cloud/waters vision with a doxology and an exhortation rhetorically addressed to his community (chap. 75). The exhortation makes explicit references to the Exodus (75:7-8) and thereby situates Baruch's words within the context of the Mosaic covenant. Then Ramiel tells him:

> . . . hear the word. . . . For you surely will depart from this earth, nevertheless not to death, but you will be preserved until the consummation of times. Go up therefore to the top of that mountain, and there will pass before you all the regions of that land, and the figure of the inhabited world, and the tops of the mountains and the depths of the valleys, and the number of the rivers, that you might see what you are leaving and where you are going. Now this all will happen after forty days. (76:2-4)

Clearly, Ramiel's announcement of the final departure of Baruch is modelled after the account of Moses' death in Deuteronomy 34. This announcement of Baruch's future is followed by his testamentary speech to his people (77:2-10).

Thus, the author of 2 Baruch has incorporated motifs from the Mosaic testamentary tradition into his work. These motifs function as part of the argument about theodicy: By establishing a typology between Baruch and Moses, the author expresses his conviction that the Mosaic covenant has not been nullified. God still keeps His promises to His people; as He once raised up Joshua to succeed Moses, so now he will continue to raise up leaders to instruct the people in the Torah.

EXCURSUS C:

THE EPISTLE OF BARUCH

In Chapter I, I indicated that there is a broad consensus that the *Epistle of Baruch* (chaps. 78:1-87:1) is an integral part of 2 Baruch.[111] On the basis of the preceding analysis of the literary structure of 2 Baruch and the exposition of its issues, I now can defend my hypothesis that 2 Baruch consists of Chapters 1-77 exclusively.

Certainly, there are a number of literary similarities between the documents. For example, the opening and closing words of the *Epistle* identify it as the letter composed by Baruch in 2 Baruch 77:

> These are the words of that epistle which Baruch the son of Neriah sent to the nine and one-half tribes. (78:1)

> And it came to pass when I had ended all the words of this epistle . . . that I folded it, and sealed it carefully, and bound it to the neck of an eagle, and dismissed and sent it. (87:1)

The description within the *Epistle* of the angelic activity against the city (chap. 80) is similar to the narrative description in 2 Baruch 6-8. Moreover, Baruch's reminder to his audience of the stipulations of the Mosaic covenant (84:1-5) echoes 2 Baruch 15-19. Finally, the statement in the *Epistle* regarding God's revelatory activity to Baruch is an accurate summary of the divine communications to Baruch throughout 2 Baruch:

> . . . I prayed . . . How long will these things endure for us?
> . . . And the Mighty One did according to the multitude of His

---

[111]See above, p. 1. For a discussion of the manuscript evidence of the *Epistle*, see Bogaert, *Apocalypse*, 1. 67-78.

mercies and the Most High according to the greatness of His
compassion, and He revealed to me the word, that I might
receive consolation, and He showed me the visions that I
should not again endure anguish, and He made known to me
the mystery of the times and the advent of the hours He
showed me. (81:2-4)

However, the presence of these similarities indicates only that the
author of the *Epistle* was acquainted with 2 Baruch. It does not necessarily indicate that the *Epistle* was an original part of 2 Baruch. In fact, the
argument that the two documents originally were distinct entities can be
defended in several ways.

The literary analysis of the structure of 2 Baruch has revealed that
the story which begins in Chapter 1 moves to its logical conclusion in
Chapter 77. Particularly significant in this context is the observation
that the structure of Block 7 (chap. 77) parallels that of Block 1 (chaps. 1-
5). This symmetry supports the position that Block 7 brings to a conclusion the story which begins in Block 1.

Moreover, a comparison of the themes of the *Epistle* with relevant
material in 2 Baruch reveals that the author of the *Epistle* has omitted
some of the main themes of 2 Baruch, embellished others, used some
motifs unknown to 2 Baruch, and contradicted an essential theme which
runs like a thread through 2 Baruch.

Certain themes essential to the unfolding of the story in 2 Baruch
are completely lacking in the *Epistle*. For example, there is no mention
of ongoing leadership under the Torah or of the identity of the *few* righteous Jews who have remained loyal to their covenantal heritage.

Other themes of 2 Baruch are embellished in the *Epistle* in ways
which distinguish them from their counterparts in 2 Baruch. For example,
the motif of God's judgment against the nations in 2 Baruch is elaborated
into a lengthy and vehement denunciation of the nations (82:3-9).
2 Baruch's understanding of God's chastening activity is embellished in the
Epistle to include the effects of the "rectitude of your fathers" and the
need to "become worthy of your fathers":

And at all times make request perseveringly and pray dili-
gently . . . that the Mighty One may be reconciled to you, and
that He may not reckon the multitude of your sins, but
remember the *rectitude of your fathers*. (84:10)

. . . that you may justify His judgment which He has decreed
against you that you should be carried away captive—for

> what you have suffered is disproportionate to what you have
> done—in order that at the last times you may be found *wor-*
> *thy of your fathers.* (78:5)

In these ways, the author of the *Epistle* embellishes themes which appear
in different ways in 2 Baruch.

The author of the *Epistle* also utilizes themes which are lacking in
2 Baruch. For example, in the *Epistle* Baruch states:

> Moreover, let this epistle be for a testimony between me and
> you, that you may remember the commandments of the
> Mighty One, and that also *there may be to me a defense* in
> the presence of Him who sent me. And remember the law
> and Zion, and the *holy land,* and your brethren, and the cove-
> nant of your fathers, and forget not the *festivals and the*
> *sabbaths.* And deliver this epistle *and the traditions of the*
> *law to your sons after you,* as also your fathers delivered
> them to you. (84:7-9)

The concept of Baruch's epistle as a "defense" for him, the inclusion of
"festivals and sabbaths," and the exhortation to "transmit the epistle and
the traditions of the law to your sons after you" all are lacking in
2 Baruch.

At the same time, one theme essential to the story of 2 Baruch is
contradicted in the *Epistle*. Throughout 2 Baruch, the author emphasizes
that the final times cannot come until all the steps in God's plan are
completed. Thus the consummation is not perceived as an imminent
reality. In contrast, in the *Epistle,* the author assures his readers that the
final times are coming imminently. For example, he states:

> For the youth of the world is past, and the strength of crea-
> tion already exhausted, and the advent of the times is very
> short, yes, they have passed by; and the pitcher is near to the
> cistern, and the ship to the port, and the course of the jour-
> ney to the city, and life to (its) consummation. (84:10)

An examination of the terminology used in the *Epistle* also indicates
that the two documents are distinct entities. A number of expressions
within the *Epistle* differ substantially from the terminology used in
2 Baruch. The people are exhorted to direct their hearts properly because
". . . we are still in the spirit and the power of our liberty" (85:7). Statements used to describe the imminence of the end times include ". . . the

youth of the world is past . . . the pitcher is near to the cistern . . . the ship is near to the port" (85:10). Judgment against the wicked is described by the phrase ". . . the way of fire, the path that brings to Gehenna" (85:13). None of these expressions is paralleled or even paraphrased in 2 Baruch.

Thus, the argument that 2 Baruch and the *Epistle* originally were distinct entities can be supported on the basis of structure, content, and terminology. At the same time, similarities between the documents indicate that the author of the *Epistle* was acquainted with 2 Baruch. The evidence seems to suggest that at some time after the composing of 2 Baruch, an unknown author utilized portions of that document and supplemented or embellished them with other traditions in order to adapt themes within 2 Baruch which were relevant to his situation. The vehemence against the Gentiles in the *Epistle* suggests that tensions between Jews and Gentiles perhaps motivated the composition of the *Epistle*.

IV

The Historical Situation
Reflected in 2 Baruch

INTRODUCTION

In Chapters II-III, I discussed the narrative world of 2 Baruch. In this chapter, I will examine what we can learn from 2 Baruch about the real world of its author. I will begin by dealing with the date of composition of the book. After examining the history of research, I will conclude that the exact date of composition is uncertain. Then I will attempt to draw out of the text clues to the author's perception of his real world. These clues will be based on two kinds of data: the portrait of Baruch in 2 Baruch and in related documents; and evidence in 2 Baruch about the situation of the author's community. In conclusion, I will make several generalizations about the contribution of 2 Baruch to an understanding of the historical situation in Palestine near the end of the first century C.E.

Throughout the chapter, I will refer to the "community to whom 2 Baruch is addressed." I am using the term "community" in a fairly loose sense to identify the recipients of 2 Baruch, and am not presupposing that they constituted an organized, clearly defined group.

DATE OF COMPOSITION

Terminus a Quo

The Problem

There is a general, if not unanimous, consensus that the author of 2 Baruch has used the destruction of Jerusalem by Babylon in 587 B.C.E. as a model for its destruction by Rome in 70 C.E.[1] Thus, the *terminus a*

---

[1] A few scholars have attempted to date 2 Baruch ca. 63 B.C.E., arguing that the document refers to the entrance of Pompey into Jerusalem. This dating was suggested first by: J. E. H. Thomson, *Books which*

quo for the composition of 2 Baruch is 70 C.E. However, attempts to fix the date of composition more precisely are hindered by two factors: the lack of unambiguous historical references in 2 Baruch; and the lack of adequate information about the history of Palestine in the years following 70 C.E.[2] The problems posed by the absence of concrete data have compelled scholars to reconstruct the date of composition on the basis of ambiguous evidence.

The History of Research

In the nineteenth century, the date of composition of 2 Baruch tended to be fixed in relationship to the date of composition of *4 Ezra*. The reference in *4 Ezra* 3:1 to ". . . the thirtieth year after the fall of Jerusalem" was interpreted as indicating a date of composition of 100 C.E. for *4 Ezra*. This date, in turn, was the criterion by which the date of 2 Baruch was determined. Scholars who believed that *4 Ezra* is dependent on 2 Baruch argued that 2 Baruch was written before 100 C.E. Conversely, scholars who were convinced that 2 Baruch is dependent on *4 Ezra* argued that 2 Baruch was composed after 100 C.E.[3]

Influenced Our Lord and His Apostles, Being a Critical View of Jewish Apocalyptic Literature (Edinburgh: T & T Clark, 1891) 255; and by M. Friedländer, *Geschichte der jüdischen Apologetik als Vorgeschichte des Christenthums* (Zurich, 1903) 151. A modern scholar sympathetic to this view is J. Hadot, "La Datation de l'Apocalypse syriaque de Baruch," *Sem* 15 (1965) 79-97. P.-M. Bogaert (*Apocalypse de Baruch* [SC 144-45; Paris: Le Cerf, 1969] 1. 270-71) has refuted this theory by noting the distinction between the profanation and the destruction of the Temple. The consensus that 2 Baruch was written after 70 C.E. is based on its character as a reaction to the destruction and on the explicit reference to the destruction in 32:4. See Bogaert (*Apocalypse*, 1. 270-95) for a concise survey of the dates proposed for the composition of 2 Baruch.

[2]See E.M. Smallwood, *The Jews Under Roman Rule* (Leiden: E.J. Brill, 1976), 331. She presents an excellent survey of this time period (331-55).

[3]See the discussion by E. Schürer, *A History of the Jewish People in the Time of Jesus Christ* (Edinburgh: T & T Clark, 1897) 3. 88-91. Schürer lists the proponents of the priority of 2 Baruch and those of the priority of 4 Ezra. He concludes that 2 Baruch was composed before 4 Ezra.

In 1911, C. Sigwalt approached the question of the date of composition from a different perspective.[4] 2 Baruch begins ". . . in the twenty-fifth year of Jeconiah, king of Judah" (1:1). The reference is problematic because Jeconiah (= Jehoiachin) reigned as king of Judah only three months before he was deported to Babylon by Nebuchadnezzar ca. 597 B.C.E. (2 Kgs 24:8-17). Sigwalt suggested that the author was referring to the twenty-fifth year after Jeconiah became king. Jeconiah began his reign in 599 or 597 B.C.E. The twenty-fifth year after that year would be 574 or 572 B.C.E.—i.e., twelve or fourteen years after the first destruction. On the basis of the typology between 587 B.C.E. and 70 C.E., Sigwalt argued that 2 Baruch was written twelve or fourteen years after the second destruction of Jerusalem—in 82 or 84 C.E.

In 1939, L. de Gry challenged Sigwalt's proposal by arguing that the "twenty-fifth year of Jeconiah" refers to the twenty-fifth year of exile, and therefore to the twenty-fifth year after the destruction of Jerusalem (i.e., 95 C.E.).[5] After comparing the beginning of 2 Baruch with that of 4 Ezra, de Gry suggested that a redacter of 2 Baruch inserted the reference to Jeconiah in order to establish the priority of 2 Baruch by dating it in 95 C.E., five years before the date of 4 Ezra. Thus, de Gry did not believe that 95 C.E. was the actual date of compostion of 2 Baruch. On the basis of his analysis of chapters 27-28, de Gry argued that 2 Baruch was written ca. 116 C.E. His argument was based on the assumption that each of the twelve parts of the last times listed in chapters 27-28 refers to a specific historical event. De Gry was convinced that the key to the identification of these events was to be found in the interpretation of 2 Baruch 28:2: ". . . for the measure and reckoning of that time are two parts, weeks of seven weeks." He interpreted the verse as indicating ninety-eight years (2 X 7 X 7). He suggested that this time period originally extended from the Battle of Actium in 31 B.C.E. (the first part of the last times) to the beginning of the Jewish War in 67 C.E. However, de Gry acknowledged a problem in this plan: according to his scheme, parts five through eleven of the last times occur after 67 C.E. He resolved this

---

[4]C. Sigwalt, "Die Chronologie der syrischen Baruchapokalypse," *BZ* 9 (1911) 397-98.

[5]L. de Gry, "La Date de la fin des temps selon les revelations ou les calculs de Pseudo-Philon et de Baruch," *RB* 48 (1939) 336-56. De Gry's assessment of Chapters 27-28 is somewhat similar to that proposed earlier by B. Violet. For a summary of de Gry's position, see Bogaert, *Apocalypse* 1. 284-93.

dilemma by suggesting that a later author added another week of years (7 X 7 years) to the 67 C.E. date, and therefore connected the twelve parts of time to his own time—116 C.E. De Gry concluded that the author of 2 Baruch, writing ca. 116 C.E., believed that the commencement of Trajan's reign signaled the beginning of the final times.

The most extensive recent discussion on the date of composition of 2 Baruch is that of P.-M. Bogaert (1969).[6] Bogaert argues that there are at least two indications that 2 Baruch was written ca. 95 C.E. Although he disagrees with most of de Gry's thesis, he concurs that de Gry was correct in suggesting that the "twenty-fifth year of Jeconiah" refers to the twenty-fifth year after the destruction of 70 C.E. (= 95 C.E.). Then, turning to the interpretation of the cloud/waters vision, he uses the reference to Manasseh's idol with five faces (64:3) to corroborate this date. After tracing the development of the legend of Manasseh's idol in various aggadic texts, Bogaert notes that the version in 2 Baruch is unusual because it emphasizes that the idol has five, rather than four, faces. He then examines traditions of this kind of idol, and determines that ca. 241 B.C.E. a five-faced idol of the cult of Ianus Quadriformis was brought to Rome. This particular cult was not at all significant until it was revived by Domitian (81-96 C.E.). Bogaert suggests that the author of 2 Baruch, writing near the end of Domitian's reign (ca. 95 C.E.), knew about this cult and incorporated it into the tradition about Manasseh in the cloud/waters vision.

Evaluation of Research

Despite the consensus that the *terminus a quo* for the writing of 2 Baruch is 70 C.E., the exact date of composition of the book has not been established in any definitive way. Indeed, there are serious flaws in most of the theories described above. The attempt to use 4 Ezra as a guide to the dating of 2 Baruch is unsatisfactory. Even if a literary relationship between the books is assumed, lack of consensus regarding the chronological priority of the books negates the value of that relationship as a guide to the dating of 2 Baruch. The attempt to interpret chapters 27-28 in terms of actual historical events is also unsatisfactory. De

---

[6]Bogaert, *Apocalypse*, 1. 272-80, 294-319.

Gry's choice of historical events is only one of several possibilities.[7] Particularly unconvincing is his method of bracketing events which do not fit his scheme and identifying them as redactions. Similarly, the suggestion that a redactor was responsible for the reference to "the twenty-fifth year of Jeconiah" rests on the unproven assumption that at some stage in the history of its transmission 2 Baruch was in competition with 4 Ezra. The argument that the "twenty-fifth year of Jeconiah" represents the twenty-fifth year of the exile is implausible. If the author wanted to indicate the twenty-fifth year of exile, he could have begun "the thirty-seventh (or thirty-ninth) year of Jeconiah." Moreover, in order to find references in 2 Baruch to an idolatrous cult in Rome, it is necessary to assume that 2 Baruch was written for a diaspora audience which would have been acquainted with Domitian's policies. This assumption requires further investigation.[8]

If we assume that the author used the "twenty-fifth year of Jeconiah" to indicate the date of composition, then C. Sigwalt's argument is the most feasible hypothesis thus far presented. It seems reasonable that one way to indicate a date of composition of a particular document would be to refer to a fixed date with which the book's readers would be familiar. The Jewish reader of 2 Baruch would have known that Jeconiah became king ca. 599-597 B.C.E. Thus, he would have known that twenty-five years after that event would have been twelve or fourteen years after the destruction. By using the destruction of 587 B.C.E. as a model for the destruction of 70 C.E., he would have concluded that the book was written in 82 or 84 C.E.[9] This hypothesis is reasonable. However, it is not definitive. Because the twenty-fifth year of Jeconiah does not coincide with 587 B.C.E., all attempts to use this datum in a 587 B.C.E./70 C.E. typology must remain conjectures. In the final analysis, the exact date of composition of 2 Baruch is uncertain.

---

[7]Ibid., 1. 291-93. Bogaert shows how the twelve parts of time could be interpreted as referring to different events than those suggested by de Gry. For another criticism of this kind of methodology, see F. M. Cross, *The Ancient Library at Qumran and Modern Biblical Studies* (Garden City: Doubleday, 1958) 159-60.

[8]See below, n. 28.

[9]My awareness of this method of indicating the date of composition is indebted to the approach of J. Goldstein, "The Apocryphal Book of 1 Baruch," *American Academy for Jewish Research* 46-47 (1979-80) 179-99.

Terminus ad Quem

The Problem

To my knowledge, all commentators of 2 Baruch have assumed that the *terminus ad quem* of its date of composition is the second Jewish revolt of 132-135 C.E. They generally have based their arguments on alleged references in 2 Baruch to certain historical events, or on allusions to 2 Baruch in later documents.

The History of Research

In 1885, F. Rosenthal attempted to show that the *terminus ad quem* of 2 Baruch is the conclusion of the diaspora revolts of 115-117 C.E. He suggested a dated of composition ca. 116 C.E., arguing that the book is a political document written as a summons to conflict at a time when Jewish rebels in the diaspora were filled with Messianic hopes.[10] In more recent times, this view has been modified by S. Zeitlin, who argues that the book was written between 117-132 C.E., and is an example of the kind of political propaganda which inspired Jews to take part in the Bar Cochba revolt.[11]

Other scholars have argued that 2 Baruch is cited in a quotation of Papias. The following quotation of Papias, recorded by Irenaeus, was perceived to be a citation of 2 Baruch 29:5:

> . . . as the elders who saw John, the disciple of the Lord,
> related that they had heard from him how the Lord used to
> teach in regard to those times, and say: The days will come
> in which vines shall grow, each having ten thousand branches,
> and in each branch ten thousand twigs, and in each true twig
> ten thousand shoots, and in each one of the shoots ten thou-
> sand clusters . . .(5.33,3).[12]

---

[10]F. Rosenthal, *Vier apokryphische Bücher aus der Zeit und Schule R. Akiba's* . . .(Leipzig: O. Schulze, 1885) 100-102.

[11]S. Zeitlin, "The Apocrypha," *JQR* 37 (1947) 239-48.

[12]Irenaeus, "Against Heresies," *The Ante-Nicene Fathers* (trans., A. Robert and J. Donaldson; Grand Rapids: Eerdmans, 1973 reprint) 1. 562-63.

On the basis of this quotation, the *terminus ad quem* for the composition of 2 Baruch was set ca. 125-30 C.E.[13]

More recently, P.-M. Bogaert has argued that the *Epistle of Barnabas* cites 2 Baruch and therefore provides the terminus ad quem for the book.[14] He lists two sets of parallels between the books:

> Again another prophet says, "And the land of Jacob shall be extolled above every land." (*Barn.* 11:14)[15]

> And the land was then beloved by the Lord, and because its inhabitants sinned not, it was glorified beyond all lands, and the city Zion then ruled over all lands and regions. (2 Baruch 61:7)

> For it is written, "And it shall come to pass, when the week is completed, the temple of God shall be built in glory in the name of the Lord." (*Barn.* 16:14)[16]

> And afterwards it (the Temple) must be renewed in glory and perfected forevermore. (2 Baruch 32:4)

On the basis of his dating of the *Epistle of Barnabas,* Bogaert uses these parallels to support his thesis that 2 Baruch was composed ca. 95 C.E.

Evaluation of the Research

None of the preceding attempts to establish the *terminus ad quem* of the composition of 2 Baruch is convincing. The argument that there are references in 2 Baruch to certain (post-70 C.E.) political events is based on the unproven assumption that the document has specific political overtones. Moreover, our knowledge of the political situation of this time period is too sketchy to isolate one of the few political crises of which we

---

[13]This position is discussed by J. Hadot, "La Datation . . . ," 80-81. Although he does not identify the scholars who take this position, he states: "Bien que *Baruch* ne soit pas cité, les spécialistes ont admis que l'allusion était évidente et que *Baruch* était connu de Papias. On peut dire que le consensus est unanime sur ce point."

[14]Bogaert, *Apocalypse,* 1. 272-80.

[15]"The Epistle of Barnabas," *The Ante-Nicene Fathers,* 1. 144. Bogaert cites the text as *Barn.* 11:9.

[16]Ibid., 147. Here Bogaert cites the text as *Barn.* 16:6.

are aware and correlate it with the writing of 2 Baruch. The attempts to find allusions to 2 Baruch in patristic writings are based on the assumption that similarity indicates dependence rather than independent appropriations of common material. With regard to the quotations cited above, this assumption is unwarranted. A variation of the material quoted by Papias appears also in *1 Enoch* 10:18-19 and in rabbinic writings.[17] It is impossible to determine its source or to trace the trajectory of its appearance in various documents. The parallels suggested by Bogaert between *Barnabas* and 2 Baruch are tenuous, to say the least. Moreover, *Barnabas* 16:14 is practically a paraphrase of *1 Enoch* 93:7; 91:13.

Thus, the *terminus ad quem* of the composition of 2 Baruch remains unknown. The book is not cited in patristic writings, and there are no sound indications that it was composed in response to political events between 115 and 135 C.E.

In summary, we lack sufficient evidence to determine the exact date of composition of 2 Baruch. Since we cannot establish the author's real world on the basis of the dating of the book, a different approach to the author's historical situation is warranted. In what follows, I will attempt to draw out of the text of 2 Baruch clues to the author's perception of his world, without trying to ascertain the year in which the book was composed.

INTERNAL EVIDENCE ABOUT THE
AUTHOR'S REAL WORLD

The Portrait of Baruch

Introduction

The practice of ascribing authorship to a pseudonymous figure was common in the time period in which 2 Baruch was composed. Moreover, the choice of a pseudonym often reflected the central concerns of the actual author.[18] Therefore, an analysis of the author's choice of "Baruch"

---

[17]For examples of rabbinc traditions similar to 2 Baruch 29:1-30:1, see *b.b. Bat.* 74b, 75a; *b. Ketub.* 111b. For a discussion, see J. Klausner, *The Messianic Idea in Israel* (New York: Macmillan Co., 1955) 343-45.

[18]For an excellent analysis of the phenomenon of pseudepigraphic writing, see B. Metzger, "Literary Forgeries and Canonical Pseudepigrapha," *JBL* 91 (1972) 3-23.

as a pseudonym may help to clarify his perception of the historical situation in which he wrote.

P.-M. Bogaert is the only major scholar to have considered this matter in any detail.[19]   He suggests that the use of the pseudonym "Baruch" is based on the tradition that Baruch was Ezra's teacher in Babylon. He presents two types of support for this thesis. The first piece of evidence is a rabbinic tradition that Baruch was Ezra's teacher. The second is the literary relationship between 4 Ezra and 2 Baruch. According to Bogaert, the similarities between the books indicate that they originated in a common milieu. The testamentary format of 2 Baruch makes that book appear to be the testament of the teacher (Baruch) to his student (Ezra).

Bogaert's thesis is not unreasonable. However, we cannot overlook other possibilities. By examining other documents in which Baruch appears and comparing them with the portrait of Baruch in 2 Baruch, we can gain further clues about why the author chose this particular pseudonym. In so doing, we will also gain clues about his perception of his real world.

Scriptural and Non-Scriptural Traditions
about Baruch

The book of Jeremiah provides the earliest reference to the figure of Baruch. There he is portrayed as the scribe of the prophet Jeremiah (Jer 36:4, 10-20; 45:1). As a scribe, he takes dictation from Jeremiah and, at Jeremiah's request, he reads the documents he has written to certain persons. These documents announce the impending destruction of Jerusalem.[20]

---

[19]Bogaert, *Apocalypse,* 1. 100-19.   The rabbinic tradition that Baruch was a teacher of Ezra in Babylon occurs in *b. Meg.* 16b and *Cant. Rab.* 5:4.

[20]The origin and function of scribes within Judaism is enigmatic because the rabbis were unclear about their identity and function and because later scholars tended to identify them with rabbis. As nearly as can be ascertained, scribes originated in the ancient world as men who could write documents. In this capacity, they became legal assistants to priests and in time supplanted priests as interpreters of the law. They continued to function primarily as legal authorities. For a further discussion of this topic, see E. Bickerman, "The Historical Foundations of Post-biblical Judaism," *The Jews: Their History, Culture, and Religion* (ed. L. Finkelstein; 2d ed.; New York: Harper and Brothers, 1949) 1. 97-99.

Baruch and Jeremiah appear together again in the *Paraleipomena of Jeremiah*.[21] In this document, as in the scriptural text, Jeremiah is the primary figure. He is characterized as prophet and priest, and he is sent to Babylon with the captives. Baruch remains in Palestine, and sixty-six years after the destruction is told to send a letter to Jeremiah detailing the conditions for the return of the exiles to Jerusalem. He does so, and Jeremiah leads the faithful Jews back to their homeland.

3 Baruch, or the *Greek Apocalypse of Baruch*, describes the revelation Baruch receives during the sixty-six year period mentioned in the *Paraleipomena of Jeremiah*.[22] In response to his questions about the destruction, Baruch is shown the "mysteries of God" in a guided tour of the five heavens. Because he has entered the hidden world and has learned that God exercises beneficent control over creation, his grief is transformed into praise. Neither the future world and time nor the eschatological restoration of Jerusalem is mentioned in this book.

The apocryphal book of 1 Baruch begins as Baruch reads a document he has written to the exiles in Babylon five years after the destruction of Jerusalem (1:1-4).[23] The main theme of this book is exile and return. The dispersion was the result of the people's sins; however, in the very near future Jerusalem's children will return to her.

In summary, all of these documents are set in the time of the first destruction and are attached to a figure living at that time. With the exception of *3 Baruch*, they all portray Baruch as a scribe, whose tasks include the writing of the documents. In Jeremiah, he records a message of impending destruction; in 1 Baruch and the *Paraleipomena of Jeremiah* he writes that return and restoration are imminent.[24]

---

[21]For a brief discussion of this book, see G. Nickelsburg, *Jewish Literature Between the Bible and the Mishnah* (Philadelphia: Fortress Press, 1981) 313-16.

[22]For a brief introduction to the book, see Nickelsburg, *Jewish Literature*, 299-303. The reference to the tradition recorded in the *Paraleipomena of Jeremiah* occurs in *3 Baruch* 1:3.

[23]See Nickelsburg, *Jewish Literature*, 109-13. I am referring to the book as "1" Baruch in order to distinguish it from the person Baruch.

[24]The name "Baruch" also appears in several other rabbinic writings. In these writings, his status as a scribe is not discussed. Rather, different opinions are presented regarding his status as a prophet. The few traditions which assert that he was indeed a prophet (e.g., *b.Meg.* 14b) also claim that he was a priest. For a discussion, see Bogaert, *Apocalypse*, 1. 104-08.

Comparison with the Portrait of Baruch
in 2 Baruch

In the final chapter of 2 Baruch (chap. 77), Baruch carries out the
scribal functions traditionally ascribed to him by writing the letters to the
diaspora. However, throughout the book he is portrayed as much more
than a scribe. He functions as a prophet who receives revelations from
God (e.g., chaps. 1-2, chap. 13), discusses those revelations with God (e.g.,
chaps. 3-5; 14-20), and communicates them to the people (e.g., 31:3-32:7;
chaps. 44-46).[25] In essence, he functions much as Jeremiah functions in
the book of Jeremiah. Moreover, Jeremiah is secondary to him, and
responds to his instructions (2:1; 9:1-10:4). The portrait of Baruch as the
scribe/prophet whose authority exceeds that of Jeremiah is one factor
distinguishing the use of the pseudonym "Baruch" in 2 Baruch from its use
in other documents.

The nature of the revelation which Baruch receives is another
factor which distinguishes the portrait of Baruch in 2 Baruch from his
portrayal in several of the other documents. The message communicated
by Baruch in 1 Baruch and the *Paraleipomena of Jeremiah* is one of imminent return and restoration. In contrast, the message Baruch receives and
communicates in 2 Baruch is that the envisioned restoration is not imminent. It will come, but only after all the steps in God's plan have been
completed.

In regard to the issue of restoration, there is a striking similarity
between 2 Baruch and Jeremiah 28-29. In Jeremiah 28, the prophet
Hananiah announces that the exile will last only two years; then the
people and the Temple vessels will be returned to Jerusalem (28:1-4, 10-
11). After he has rebuked Hananiah, Jeremiah writes to the exiles in
Babylon and encourages them not to anticipate an imminent return. The
exile will end, but only after seventy years have passed (29:4-14). Thus,
both Jeremiah 28-29 and 2 Baruch emphasize that hopes of immediate
restoration are premature.

---

[25]The characterization of Baruch as a prophetic figure is apparent
already in chap. 1: The Word of God comes to him in a certain year of a
king, describes the problem, and announces the divine response. Cf. Jeremiah 1:2; Amos 1:1. For a discussion of the prophetic mode of communication, see G. von Rad, *Old Testament Theology* (New York: Harper &
Row, 1965) 2. 129-35. The process whereby prophetic functions came to
be ascribed to scribes is described by M. Hengel, *Judaism and Hellenism*
(Philadelphia: Fortress Press, 1974) 1. 131-38. Hengel observes the
pivotal role of ben Sira in this development.

At the same time, a striking difference between these chapters of Jeremiah and 2 Baruch becomes apparent when Jeremiah 29:6 is compared with 2 Baruch 1:4:

> *Seek* the welfare of any city to which I [God] have carried you off, and pray to the Lord for it; on its welfare your welfare will depend. (Jer 29:6)

> I [God] will scatter this people among the Gentiles, that they might do good for the Gentiles. And my people will be chastened, and they will *seek* the prosperity of their times. (2 Baruch 1:4)

Jeremiah exhorts the people to settle down in Babylon for the seventy year period. Since the return cannot be rushed, they are to *seek* the welfare of the cities in which they are located in the interim. In contrast, the author of 2 Baruch does not tell the exiles to seek the welfare of the cities to which they are sent. Instead, he states that eventually they will *seek* the prosperity of their times.[26] The subsequent discussions make it clear that those "times" are the final eschatological times, which will occur only after God's plan has been completed.[27] Thus, here the author of 2 Baruch has neatly changed the sense of Jeremiah 29:6 to replace the hope of historical restoration with the anticipation of the consummation of the times.

In summary, Jeremiah and 2 Baruch both assert that there will be a restoration, but that it is not imminent. In this regard, 2 Baruch counters the promise of 1 Baruch by returning to the message of Jeremiah. However, 2 Baruch also moves beyond the position of Jeremiah by asserting that the restoration will occur in the eschaton. The *Paraleipomena of Jeremiah* continues the traditions of 1 Baruch, rather that of 2 Baruch. *3 Baruch* differs from all these documents; consolation occurs as Baruch takes a heavenly journey and learns that God exercises beneficent control

---

[26] There is a difference between Jeremiah's perception of "seeking the welfare of the city" and 2 Baruch's notion of "doing good for the Gentiles." Jeremiah lacks the sense of thereby allowing the Gentiles to do more sins which seems to be part of 2 Baruch's concern. See above, pp. 46-47.

[27] The eschatological dimensions of 2 Baruch 1:4 are clearly evident in Block 2 (2D—13:3-10; 19:4-8), where the terms "chasten" and "prosperity" both are used with reference to the consummation of times.

over creation. The use of the pseudonym "Baruch" enables the author of 2 Baruch to counter the message of 1 Baruch by returning to the Jeremianic tradition about the length of the exile. At the same time, he departs from this tradition by declaring that the restoration will occur at the eschaton.

The Situation of the Author's Community

In 2 Baruch, we are given a glimpse of how one author has created a narrative world based on the events of 587 B.C.E. in order to respond to the situation contronting a community in Palestine in the years following 70 C.E.[28] On the basis of clues which have emerged in the preceding chapters, we can make some generalizations about the author's perception of the real world of these people.

We lack sufficient evidence to determine whether and to what extent the community addressed by the author was a formally organized, well-defined group. However, we can sense "in group/out group" dynamics at work throughout the book. The author portrays the people to whom he writes as a faithful minority within the broader Jewish community. He defines this community of the *few* as "Israel," arguing that only these Jews, and the Gentiles who have chosen to associate with them, have remained loyal to the Mosaic covenant. These people are contrasted with the *many* Jews, whose main transgression seems to have been assimilation to the ways of the Gentiles. Although the evidence is inconclusive, there is some indication that this community may have regarded the Temple cult as defiled prior to the destruction. The author's use of the story

---

[28]Bogaert (*Apocalypse*, 1. 335-52) argues that 2 Baruch was written in Palestine for a diaspora audience. His main support for this position is the *Epistle of Baruch*. I have already given evidence which suggests that the *Epistle* is not a part of 2 Baruch (see above, Excursus C). However, even if the reference to the sending of letters to the diaspora in *2 Baruch* 77 is accepted as support for Bogaert's position, an important question remains: Does the reference indicate that the message of 2 Baruch is directed primarily to a diaspora audience; or does it indicate that the message is authoritative for all Jews, including those in the diaspora? We lack sufficient data to give a definitive answer to this question. However, a Palestinian audience is suggested by the questions raised by Baruch throughout the book and by the interaction between him and his community.

about Abraham and Sodom and of the legend about Manasseh is particularly significant in this context (see above, Excursus A).[29]

As he surveys the situation of his community in the years of chaos following 70 C.E., the author struggles with the question of whether "Israel" (i.e., the faithful *few*) can survive at all. Thus, the problem raised in his own time is the continued efficacy of the covenants God made with His people in the past. This problem permeates the question/answer format in which the author probes the theological ramifications of the destruction. Its resolution permeates his attempts to apply the theological data to the practical needs of his community in their real world.

Apparently, one of these needs was a concern about continuity in the teaching office of the community. There are several clues about the nature of this teaching office. As noted above, the scribe Baruch functions as the prophetic leader of his community Moreover, the people perceive that he is the one remaining link between them and God. Only Baruch has access to Jerusalem, the location of God's revelation to His people. Thus, from the people's perspective, if Baruch departs from them, these revelations will cease. This, however, is not their entire problem. Their question "where shall we seek the Torah, and who will distinguish for us between death and life?" (46:3) implies that, as scribe/prophet, Baruch's work also includes interpreting the Torah for them. Thus, from the people's perspective, if Baruch departs from them, even the Torah will be ineffective to help them because there will be no one to interpret it for them. Baruch resolves this dilemma by transferring the teaching leadership of the community from himself to his successors and promising that the Torah will continue to spawn its own teachers as long as time endures. These interactions between Baruch and his people are a valuable indicator of the kind of teaching office envisioned by the community for whom 2 Baruch was composed. These people sought the kind of leadership which could interpret God's will for them in terms of the blessings and curses of the covenant. Moreover, they may have envisioned such leadership as a quasi-prophetic office. Perhaps the author is assuring them that

---

[29]Interestingly, in 2 Baruch the laments over the destruction of the Temple never refer to the atonement made possible through the Temple sacrifices. Perhaps this is another indication that the author had a low regard for the Temple cult. For a discussion of the Temple's role in atonement and the crisis caused by the cessation of its activities, see G. F. Moore, *Judaism in the First Centuries of the Christian Era* (Cambridge: Harvard University Press, 1927-30) 1. 497-506.

new "scribe/prophets" ("shepherds"—77:13, 16) will continue to arise for them even in the present chaotic times.

In addition to dealing with the issue of whether time is running out for "Israel," the author also repeatedly discusses the theme of "how long" until the final times occur. The lengthy discussion about the steps in God's plan indicates that the delay in the consummation was a problem for the community he addresses.[30]

A striking feature of 2 Baruch is the sense of grief over the destruction. The vividness with which this grief is expressed indicates that the author is writing to his community at a time when grief over the destruction is still acute. However, enough time has elapsed so that he can exhort them to cease mourning over the past and can assure them that they can face the present in confidence of a better future.

From the perspective of the story, the book which records Baruch's revelations and his encounters with his people is finally his legacy to his community. By portraying Baruch as if he were Abraham and Moses, the author gives the authority of these figures to Baruch's legacy. Thus, the message of God's covenant fidelity is buttressed by a typology between the book's main character and the men with whom the covenant originally was made. Moreover, Baruch's decision to send a letter to the exiles in Babylon and to the nine and one-half tribes indicates that his legacy is authoritative for all faithful descendants of the twelve tribes of Israel, including those who are scattered throughout the diaspora.

After all is said and done, the author's perception of his historical situation is quite positive. Because he is convinced that God remains in a covenant relationship with His faithful people, he can encourage his community to cease mourning over the past and to live in the present in the certain hope that they will survive in this world and will gain entrance into the future world.

CONCLUSION

On the basis of the preceding data, we can make several generalizations about the contributions of 2 Baruch to an understanding of the historical situation in Palestine at the end of the first century C.E. In

---

[30]Here I am assuming that the answer to the question of "how long?" is formulated in response to the real world of the community rather than to the narrative world of the story. The repeated emphasis on the continued existence of the community in this world indicates that the author does not expect the consummation to occur in the near future.

2 Baruch, we discover the existence of some type of community of which we have no knowledge from other documents. The efforts of the author to define this community in contradistinction to other Jews suggests that it was one of a number of such communities surviving in Palestine after the destruction. Like the Qumran community, it seems to have been critical of the Temple cult; unlike Qumran, it does not seem to have been a priestly group. Like the later rabbinic schools, it emphasized the importance of interpretation of the Torah; however, its perception of its leaders does not really fit the rabbinic mold. There are indications that this community may have envisioned their leaders as scribal/prophetic figures.[31]

The emphasis throughout 2 Baruch on God's covenant with Israel illustrates the way in which this community relied on the Scriptures in order to interpret their historical situation. These people apparently felt a great sense of loss when Jerusalem was destroyed. They seem to have taken a practical, rather than speculative, approach to the crisis precipitated by that destruction. Moreover, the stress on "time" throughout 2 Baruch reveals that Christians were not the only persons puzzled by the delay of a parousia.[32]

The contribution of 2 Baruch to an understanding of the historical situation in Palestine at the end of the first century C.E. can be summarized in one word—diversity. Contrary to what scholars have sometimes assumed, the response of the Jewish community to the events of 70 C.E. was by no means homogeneous.[33] As we will see in Chapter V, 2 Baruch provides one of a variety of responses to these events. It illustrates for us the way in which one particular community of Jews attempted to use their Scriptures in order to interpret their present situation and to plot a course for their future.

---

[31] The scribal/prophetic function of these leaders raises significant questions about the author's attitude toward the cessation of prophecy. For a summary of the traditional position that prophecy ceased with the deaths of Haggai, Zachariah, and Malachi, see Moore, *Judaism* 1. 421-22.

[32] E.g., 2 Pet 3:3-18.

[33] G. F. Moore (*Judaism*) is a primary proponent of this assumption. He argues that the rabbinic form of Judaism is the only "normative" form of Judaism to survive the destruction of 70 C.E. For a generally excellent survey of competing tendencies within Judaism after 70 C.E., see J. Neusner, *Judaism: The Evidence of the Mishnah* (Chicago: University of Chicago Press, 1981) 5-14, 25-44. Unfortunately, Neusner treats Baruch and 2 Baruch as if they express a similar viewpoint. Thus, he misses completely the significant differences between them.

V

A Comparison of 2 Baruch
with Related Documents

INTRODUCTION

In this chapter, I will compare 2 Baruch with other responses to the events of 70 C.E. The similarities and differences between these documents and 2 Baruch will highlight the uniqueness of 2 Baruch. The comparison also will enable us to make several generalizations about the situation in Palestine near the end of the first century C.E.

The four Jewish documents considered in this study—*The Biblical Antiquities* of Pseudo-Philo, 4 Ezra, the *Apocalypse of Abraham,* and the *Paraleipomena of Jeremiah*—were chosen because they all respond in some way to the events of the years ca. 70 C.E.[1] The one Christian document—the Gospel of Matthew—was selected because it too responds to these events and raises some of the same questions as are found in 2 Baruch.

The analysis of each of these documents is limited to three specific questions: (1) What biblical event or theme is used by the author to establish the narrative world of his account? (2) What questions are formulated on the basis of this event or theme? (3) How are these questions resolved? The answers to these questions will be compared to relevant portions of 2 Baruch. In conclusion, I will summarize what we can learn from these documents about the uniqueness of 2 Baruch and about various responses to the situation in Palestine in the years following 70 C.E.

---

[1]A possible exception is Pseudo-Philo, which may have been written shortly before the destruction. See below, n. 3. Bibliographical information on all of the books except Matthew is available in J. Charlesworth, *The Pseudepigrapha and Modern Research, With a Supplement,* (SCS7; Chico: Scholars Press, 1981).

PSEUDO-PHILO AND 2 BARUCH

Introduction

The *Biblical Antiquities* of Pseudo-Philo (*LAB*) is a retelling of the biblical history from Adam to the death of Saul.[2] Portions of the scriptural account are quoted, paraphrased, expanded, compressed, or omitted. In addition, prayers, speeches, and new stories are interpolated into the biblical text. An elaborated and embellished counterpart to the book of Judges constitutes the major part of the document.

The exact date of composition of Pseudo-Philo is unknown. The generally accepted *terminus ad quem* is the Bar Cochba revolt of 132 C.E. The earliest date usually suggested is the turbulent years shortly before or after the destruction of Jerusalem in 70 C.E.[3]

Analysis

The biblical basis of Pseudo-Philo is the pattern of sin/punishment/repentance/deliverance, particularly as it is developed in the book of Judges. Central to the account is the appearance of new leaders in times of crisis to deliver Israel from the nations who are oppressing her. The leadership of the judge Cenez (chaps. 25-28) is a good example of the way in which the author utilizes his biblical model.[4]

---

[2]For a helpful introduction to the book, see G. Nickelsburg, *Jewish Literature Between the Bible and the Mishnah* (Philadelphia: Fortress Press, 1981) 265-68. The primary critical editions and translations of the text are: M. R. James, *The Biblical Antiquities of Philo* (London: SPCK, 1917; reprinted in 1971 with a lengthy prolegomenon by L. Feldman); D. Harrington, J. Cazeaux, C. Perrot, P.-M. Bogaert, *Pseudo-Philon: Les Antiquites Bibliques* (SC 229-30; Paris: Le Cerf, 1976).

[3]James, *Biblical Antiquities*, 30-33; Harrington, *Pseudo-Philon* 2.78; Bogaert, *Apocalypse*, 1. 252-58; Nickelsburg, *Jewish Literature*, 267-68.

There is no agreement regarding whether the destruction of 70 C.E. is mentioned explicitly in Pseudo-Philo. There are two possible references to it. In 19:7, Moses sees the place where Israel will serve God until it is destroyed after 740 years. In 26:13, the destruction of the Temple is mentioned explicitly; however, it is unclear whether the reference is to the first or second Temple.

[4]For an excellent survey of all the leading figures in Pseudo-Philo, see G. Nickelsburg, "Good and Bad Leaders in Pseudo-Philo's *Liber Antiquitatum Biblicarum*," *Ideal Figures in Ancient Judaism* (eds. G. Nickelsburg and J. Collins; Chico: Scholars Press, 1980) 49-65. The

Cenez appears (25:1-2) in a time of national crisis: Joshua has died, the people are leaderless, and the Philistines are approaching. At God's command, the people draw lots to determine a new leader, and Cenez is chosen. The *sin* part of the pattern emerges as Cenez immediately summons all the tribes to appear before him so that the sins of the Israelites who are defiled can be discovered (25:3-13). Implied in the summons is the conviction that the national crisis is a *punishment* for these sins. After the sinners have *confessed* these transgressions and are punished (25:4-26:15),[5] Cenez *delivers* the people from their enemies in a series of military victories (chap. 27). In a prayer prior to his single-handed battle against the Philistines, Cenez confidently asserts that even if he dies, God will not allow Israel to be destroyed (27:7). When Cenez' death approaches (28:1-2), he exhorts the people to remain loyal to the covenant. Phineas then shares with the people the revelation which his father Eliezer the priest received (28:3-4). According to the revelation, God both foreordained the election of Israel and also foresaw that the people would forsake Him. When the people and Cenez ask God if He will destroy Israel (28:5), Cenez is given an ecstatic vision, which he recounts as he receives it (28:6-9). Although the meaning of the vision is obscure, it seems to imply that, while God will not let Israel be destroyed, her problems will be resolved ultimately only on an eschatological level.[6] After he has awakened from his vision, Cenez dies (28:10).

Because it is a good example of the biblical pattern used by the author to establish his narrative world, the story of Cenez provides valuable clues to the question which the author is addressing. The problem which runs through the entire story of Cenez is the oppression of Israel by foreign nations. The repeated emphasis on this problem throughout the

---

following summary of Cenez' life is based in part on the comments on pp. 54-55.

The sin/punishment/repentance/deliverance pattern is expressed more often in leaders' speeches than in their narrative activities. I have chosen to use the whole story of Cenez as an example in order to give the reader a sense of how the story of Pseudo-Philo unfolds.

[5]In this particular instance, repentance does not lead to the deliverance of those who have confessed their sins. They are killed as punishment. However, because their confession has made it possible to identify and destroy the causes of sin within the community, the remainder of the people are delivered from the enemy.

[6]Nickelsburg, "Good and Bad Leaders," 54-55.

book identifies it as the primary crisis to which the author is responding.[7]
On this basis, the central question addressed in Pseudo-Philo can be stated
as follows: "Will Israel survive the present oppression by the nations?".

In addition to illustrating the question which is being addressed in
Pseudo-Philo, the story of Cenez also reveals the resolution suggested by
the author. Cenez' prayer and vision and Phineas' revelation reiterate
another theme which is repeated throughout the book: God chose Israel
prior to the creation of the world; although He will punish her for her sins,
He will never abandon her by allowing her to be destroyed.[8] Thus, the
author uses the sin/punishment/repentance/deliverance pattern in order to
explain what has happened and to reassure his community that they will
survive the present crisis. God remains loyal to His covenant commitment to them.

Throughout Pseudo-Philo, God's covenant fidelity is manifest
through the leadership of Cenez and other men and women like him.
These persons frequently appear in times of national crisis, give speeches
which extol God's faithfulness and exhort the people to obey the Torah,
and deliver the people from the nations who are oppressing them. Not all
leaders, however, exert a positive influence. Some, like Gideon (chaps.
35-36) and Jair (chap. 38), practice idolatry and thereby lead the people
astray. The contrasts between the good and the bad leaders seem to
indicate that Pseudo-Philo believes that the moral uprightness of the
leaders of a nation is an important element in the moral fiber of that
nation.[9]

Comparison with 2 Baruch

Pseudo-Philo and 2 Baruch both deal with the question of the survival of the Jewish community in the troubled years ca. 70 C.E. In both
documents, the present crisis is attributed to the people's sins. Both
books emphasize that God remains loyal to His covenant commitment to
His people, despite their oppression by the nations. Both books also assert

---

[7]Nickelsburg, *Jewish Literature*, 265-68. He cites the following
verses: 9:3; 12:8; 18:10-11; 19:9; 30:4; 35:3; 49:3.

[8]E.g., 18:10-12; 21:4; 23:10-14; 28:4-10; 30:2; 32:1-4; 35:2-4; 39:6;
53:8-9.

[9]For other examples of good and bad leaders, see Nickelsburg, "Good
and Bad Leaders," 50-62. See also Nickelsburg, *Jewish Literature*, 266-
67. Cf. 2 Baruch 64-65, where Manasseh's idolatry results in God's decision to allow the destruction and dispersion.

that submission to the Torah is essential to the community's survival, and both promise that God will continue to raise up leaders for His people. The most striking similarity between the books is the way in which they formulate the question of the community's survival in terms of ongoing leadership. It should be noted, however, that there are a variety of kinds of leaders in Pseudo-Philo (e.g., warriors, prophets, men who serve as examples by their deeds). In 2 Baruch, leadership is envisioned primarily in terms of interpretation of the Torah.

The primary difference between the books is the narrative world chosen as a setting for the development of the primary issues. The author of 2 Baruch uses the destruction of 587 B.C.E. as the basis from which to raise and resolve questions formulated in response to the destruction of Jerusalem in 70 C.E. These questions are variations on one major question: Have the covenants God made with Abraham and Moses been nullified? The author of Pseudo-Philo uses the biblical pattern of sin/punishment/repentance/deliverance as the basis from which to raise and resolve similar questions.

There also are several secondary differences between the books. Pseudo-Philo lacks 2 Baruch's concern with the distinction between the *few* and the *many* Jews. Also missing in Pseudo-Philo is the implicit criticism of the Temple cult which seems to permeate 2 Baruch. There is, however, an emphasis on the problem of idolatry among the people and some of their leaders. Finally, the delay in the consummation does not seem to pose the problem for the author of Pseudo-Philo that it does for the author of 2 Baruch.

4 EZRA AND 2 BARUCH

Introduction

4 Ezra is a Jewish apocalypse which, in its present form, comprises chapters 3-14 of the Christian document 2 Esdras.[10] E. Breech has argued convincingly that the structure of the book is constituted by the narrative of Ezra's movement from grief to consolation. This movement occurs within a seven-episode format.[11] The first three episodes (3:1-

---

[10]For a concise introduction to the book, see Nickelsburg, *Jewish Literature*, 287-94.

[11]E. Breech, "These Fragments I have Shored against My Ruins: The Form and Function of 4 Ezra," *JBL* 92 (1973) 267-74.

9:25) are conversations between Ezra and the angel Uriel about theodicy. The fourth episode (9:26-10:59) consists of Ezra's prayer and of the vision he receives of the heavenly Zion. Episodes 5-6 (chaps. 11-13) contain two visions of the end-time and their interpretations, while Episode 7 (chap. 14) consists of Ezra's encounter with the people and his final activities.

There are no explicit references within 4 Ezra to the exact date of its composition. However, there is a general consensus that it was written near the end of the first century C.E. This consensus is based on the opening reference to the "thirtieth year after the fall of Jerusalem" (3:1).[12]

Analysis

The destruction of Jerusalem by Babylon in 587 B.C.E. provides the basis of the narrative world of 4 Ezra. The book begins thirty years after this event, as Ezra sits on his bed in Babylon and reflects about the desolation of Zion and the prosperity of Babylon (3:1-2).[13]

As Ezra contemplates the history of mankind from the time of Adam to the present, he expresses the type of questions raised for him by the destruction:

> . . . You gave the commandments of the Torah to the Israel-
> ites, the race of Jacob. But you did not take away their
> wicked heart and enable your Torah to bear fruit in them.
> For the first man, Adam, was burdened with a wicked heart;
> he sinned and was overcome, and not only he but all his
> descendants. So the weakness became inveterate. Although
> Your Torah was in Your people's hearts, a rooted wickedness
> was there too; so that the good came to nothing, and what
> was bad persisted. Years went by, and . . . You raised up . . .
> David. You told him to build the city that bears Your name. .
> . . [After many years] the inhabitants of the city went astray,
> behaving just like Adam and all his line; for they had the
> same wicked heart. And so You gave Your city over to Your
> enemies.

---

[12]For a summary of suggested dates, see Michael Stone, *Features of the Eschatology of 4 Ezra* (Harvard Ph.D., 1965) 1-11; E. Schürer, *A History of the Jewish People in the Time of Jesus Christ* (Edinburgh: T & T Clark, 1897) 3. 99-113.

[13]Throughout this analysis and comparison, it will be evident that the authors of 4 Ezra and 2 Baruch seem to be utilizing similar traditional material. Here, cf. 2 Baruch 11:1-2.

> I said to myself: Perhaps those in Babylon lead better lives and that is why they conquered Zion. But when I arrived here, I saw more wickedness that I could reckon. . . . My heart sank, because I saw how You tolerate sinners and spare the godless; how You have destroyed Your own people, but protected Your enemies. You have given no hint whatever to anyone how to understand Your ways. (3:19-31)

Throughout his subsequent conversations with the angel Uriel (Episodes 1-3), Ezra repeats and elaborates the accusation contained in this quotation: God's demands on Israel are unjust and His method of humiliating Israel before the nations is unfair. However, Ezra's concern is not limited to the present status of Israel and the nations. He also complains that the very structure of creation prevents almost anyone from attaining life.[14] His frustration culminates in the statement of anguish:

> But this is my point, my first point and my last: how much better it would have been if the earth had never produced Adam at all, or, since it has done so, if he had been restrained from sinning! For what good does it do us all to live in misery now and have nothing but punishment to expect after death? O Adam, what have you done? Your sin was not your fall alone; it was ours also, the fall of all your descendants. What good is the hope of eternity, in the wretched and futile state to which we have come; or the prospect of dwelling in health and safety, when we have lived such evil lives? (7:116-20)[15]

In summary, Ezra's grief over the destruction of Jerusalem is expressed in various accusations directed to God. He argues that the propensity to sin with which each individual is born makes it impossible for almost anyone attain life.

Throughout Episodes 1-3, Uriel responds to Ezra's accusations by defending God and describing the signs of the final times. The defense of

---

[14]For a detailed examination of this theme in the dialogues, see W. Harnisch, *Verhängnis und Verheissung der Geschichte: Untersuchungen zum Zeit- und Geschichtsverständnis im 4. Buch Esra und in der syr. Baruchapokalypse* (FRLANT 97; Göttingen: Vandenhoeck & Ruprecht, 1969).

[15]Cf. the references to the results of Adam's sin in 2 Baruch: 17:1-4; 23:4; 48:42-47; 54:15, 19; 56:5-6. Cf. also Rom 5:12ff. and *3 Baruch* 4:8-17.

God is based on the incomprehensibility of His ways (4:1-21), His love for Israel and creation (5:31-40; 8:47), and His method of administering justice.[16] Regarding God's justice, Uriel states:

> He said to me: Such is the lot of Israel. It was for Israel that I made the world, and when Adam transgressed my decrees the creation came under judgment. The entrances to this world were made narrow, painful, and arduous, few and evil, full of perils and grinding hardship. But the entrances to the greater world are broad and safe, and lead to immortality. All men must therefore enter this narrow and futile existence; otherwise they can never attain the blessings in store. (7:11-14)

> Better that many now living should be lost, than that the Torah God has set before them should be despised God has given clear instructions for all men when they come into this world, telling them how to attain life and how to escape punishment. But the ungodly have refused to obey him; they have set up their own empty ideas, and planned deceit and wickedness; they have even denied the existence of the Most High and have not acknowledged his ways. They have rejected his Torah and refused his promises, they have neither put faith in His decrees nor done what He commands. Therefore, Ezra, emptiness for the empty, fullness for the full! (7:20-25)

> It was with conscious knowledge that the people of this world sinned, and that is why torment awaits them; they received the commandments but did not keep them, they accepted the Torah but violated it. What defence will they be able to make at the judgment, what answer at the last day? (7:72-73)

Uriel never denies that the attainment of salvation is difficult; however, he repeatedly argues that it is possible. Moreover, he concludes the conversation in Episode 3 by emphasizing how God has labored to save those few persons who are righteous (9:17-22).

In each of his conversations with Ezra, Uriel attempts to shift the discussion from the present to the final times (4:26–5:13; 6:1-34; 9:1-

---

[16]E.g. 7:3-25, 70-74, 127-131; 8:55-62; 9:18-22.

16).[17] He repeatedly assures Ezra that the end of this age is coming soon, although it cannot be rushed, and he promises Ezra that he and those persons like him are destined for glory (8:51-55). The function of these references to the final times becomes clearer when Episodes 4-6 are examined.

Episode 4 (9:26-10:59) begins as Ezra leaves his room and goes to a field called Ardat (9:26). There he sees three visions, each of which is interpreted for him. These visions enable him to move from grief to consolation, despite the fact that his questions remain unanswered. The prologue to the first vision is Ezra's encounter with a grieving woman (9:38-10:24). After Ezra tells her she should cease mourning for her son in order to grieve over Zion, she is transformed into the heavenly Zion. Ezra is allowed to enter the heavenly city and to look at its buildings (10:25-55). The second and third visions and their interpretations (eagle vision—11:1-12:39; the man from the sea vision—chap. 13) deal primarily with the Messiah's victory over the nations[18] at the final time.

These visions, coupled with Uriel's earlier descriptions of the signs and events of the final times, enable Ezra to move from grief to consolation. G. Nickelsburg summarizes the "answers" which make possible this movement to consolation:

> The writer [of 4 Ezra] . . . finds two answers to this line of questioning. The first, which is not totally different from the book of Job, is no answer at all. God simply pulls rank. . . . In His second answer God takes up the traditional apocalyptic response. He does not explain why He tolerates sin but rather directs the seer's attention to His solution of the problem:

---

[17]Cf. 2 Baruch chaps. 24-30; 48:29-41; chaps. 70-74. The process by which the world moves to its end is described in much more elaborate detail in 4 Ezra than in 2 Baruch. The extensive use of the pregnancy motif in 4 Ezra is an example of the differences between the two books in this regard. The requirement for the advent of the consummation is another example of differences between the books. According to 2 Baruch 23:4-5, the full number of the souls of *all mankind* must be born ·prior to the consummation. According to 4 Ezra 4:33-37, the number of souls of *the righteous* must be completed prior to the end. See Harnisch, *Verhängnis,* 276-87.

[18]Actually, the eagle vision (11:1-12:35) refers to the specific nation Rome, while the vision of the man from the sea (13:1-52) refers to all nations. God explains to Ezra (12:10-11) that the eagle represents the fourth kingdom in the vision of Daniel (Dan 7).

the coming judgment and the beginning of a new age which is
free from the troubles Adam brought into the present age.
The function of the visions in chaps 9-13 is to assure the seer
that this age is coming and that it will come soon.   At the
same time, material in the dialogues reminds the reader that
the time of the eschaton can not be shortened.[19]

In addition to the conversations about theodicy and the visions of the
future, Episodes 1-6 also contain two brief encounters between Ezra and
members of his community. In both encounters (5:16-19; 12:40-49), the
people or their leader express the fear that Ezra is abandoning them.
Ezra's response is limited to the assurance that neither God nor he has
forgotten them. He does not communicate to them the revelations he has
received.[20]   Moreover, immediately prior to the second encounter, he
receives interesting instructions about the communication of these revelations:

> What you [Ezra] have seen you must therefore write in a book
> and deposit it in a hiding-place. You must also disclose these
> secrets to those of your people whom you know to be wise
> enough to understand them and to keep them safe. (12:37-38)

These instructions reveal a division between the *wise* and the *many* within
Ezra's community. The wise elite can understand the esoteric knowledge
Ezra has gained; the remainder of the community simply hear that they
have not been forgotten.[21]
    Episode 7 contains Ezra's final encounter with his community.
Here the distinction between the *wise* and the *many* again is evident. The
Episode begins with an Ezra/Moses typology (14:1ff.). The voice which
once addressed Moses from a bush now tells Ezra that he, like Moses, has
received public and secret revelation. After Ezra hears that he will be
taken from the earth (14:9-18), he asks that first he may be allowed to
write down for the people everything which is in the Torah. Since the

---

[19]Nickelsburg, *Jewish Literature*, 292-94.
[20]Cf. the encounters between Baruch and his people (2 Baruch 31-
34, 44-47).
[21]There is nothing surprising in the statement that only persons with
certain intellectual qualifications can understand the revelations Ezra has
received. Throughout the first three episodes, the intellectual component
of Ezra's grief is emphasized repeatedly (4:12; 5:39-40; 7:62-64).

Torah was burned in fire,[22] he perceives that he is the last link between the Torah and the people (14:19-22).

God gives permission to Ezra to carry out this plan and tells him to gather five men skilled in writing (14:23-26). Ezra does so, and summons all the people to hear a final speech (14:27-36). The speech is based on the biblical sin/punishment/repentance/deliverance pattern. It culminates in the promise that the righteous will receive mercy at the judgment. Neither Ezra's earlier accusations nor the revelations he has received are mentioned.

After the final encounter with his people, Ezra and assistants go to the field. Ezra is given a liquid to drink which enables him to dictate books without ceasing for forty days (14:37-44). The book concludes as God gives Ezra a final set of instructions;

> . . . the Most High spoke to me. *Make public* the books you write first, He said, to *be read by good and bad alike.* But the last seventy books are to be *kept back,* and *given to none but the wise among your people.* They contain a stream of understanding, a fountain of wisdom, a flood of knowledge. (14:45-47)

Comparison with 2 Baruch

Much of the research on 2 Baruch has been done in conjunction with an examination of 4 Ezra. A number of scholars have argued that one of the books is dependent upon the other.[23] W. Harnisch is more cautious in his appraisal of the relationship between the books:

> Die Interpretation der bisher berücksichtigten Texte aus 4 Esr und sBar hat den Nachweis dafür erbracht, daß beiden Apokalypsen—ungeachtet enzelner, sachlich unerheblicher Divergenzen—ein und dieselbe theologische Gesamtkonseption

---

[22]This motif is alien to 2 Baruch. Throughout the book, the existence and availability of the Torah is assumed. From the community's perspective, the crisis precipitated by the destruction is that of leadership rather than loss of the Torah itself.

[23]Schürer (*History,* 3.89-91) lists the proponents of both sides of the dependence issue. For other discussions, see G. H. Box, "Introduction to 4 Ezra," *APOT,* 2. 553ff.; R. H. Charles, "Introduction to 2 Baruch," *APOT,* 2. 476-77. Other books which examine the literary relationship include: Nickelsburg, *Jewish Literature,* 288-93; Harnisch, *Verhängnis.*

zugrunde liegt. . . . Die unverkennbare sachlich Verwandt-
schaft beider Schriften legt die Vermutung nahe, daß sie
demselben Traditionsbereich angehören und das Selbstver-
ständnis einer bestimmten Gruppe des Spätjudentums (der
Zeit nach 70 p. Chr.) repräsentieren.[24]

The findings of the dissertation tend to support the argument that
there is a literary relationship between the books. Terminological and
thematic similarities indicate that the authors quite probably were utilizing a common source of traditional material.[25]   More importantly, the
literary structure of both books is determined by a narrative frame in
which the main character moves from grief to consolation.[26]   In both
instances, a variety of literary sub-units are clustered and arranged in
certain patterns in order to deal with the theological implications of the
events of 70 C.E. Thus, the relationship between the two books involves
much more than appropriations of common traditional material. There
are striking similarities between the ways the authors have structured
their documents from their beginning to their conclusion. To my knowledge, no comparisons of 4 Ezra and 2 Baruch have taken into account this
similar literary structure. Certainly, it is one datum which needs to be
considered in any examination of the nature of the literary relationship
between the two books.

The presence of a similar literary structure, however, does not
imply that the books are addressing the same questions. In fact, there are
at least five indications that 4 Ezra and 2 Baruch are controlled by different agendas, and thus represent significantly different responses to the
events of 70 C.E.

(1) Although both books use the destruction of 587 B.C.E. as a
model for the destruction of 70 C.E., the relationship of the main character to his fictional setting in time differs significantly. Baruch witnesses

---

[24]Harnisch, *Verhängnis,* 240.

[25]A number of terminological similarities have already been noted.
For a list of suggested terminological parallels, see R. H. Charles, *Apoc-
alypse of Baruch* (London: Black, 1896), 170-71; Nickelsburg, *Jewish
Literature,* 288-93.

[26]This is precisely the point at which Bogaert (*Apocalypse,* 1. 58-76)
flounders in his attempt to use the seven-episode structure of 4 Ezra as a
model for the structure of 2 Baruch. The story, not the episode divisions,
is the key element in assessing the literary relationship between the
books.

the destruction and *immediately* reacts to it. He laments the desolation of Zion and raises questions about the concrete implications of the destruction for the future of Israel and of the nations. He does not speculate about the theoretical implications of the event.

In contrast, we first encounter Ezra in Babylon *thirty years after the destruction*. The desolation of Zion and the prosperity of Babylon form the basis of his theoretical reflections about the effects of the evil heart on Adam's descendants (3:1ff.) While Baruch laments the particular event, Ezra probes the universal implications of the human weakness (i.e., the "evil heart") which he believes was responsible for the event.

(2) As might be expected in view of their different relationships to their fictional settings in time, the responses of Baruch and Ezra to the destruction differ significantly. Baruch argues that God's method of administering justice in this particular situation is ineffective, and he is impatient with God's failure to manifest His power to the nations immediately. The individual's ability to fulfill the Torah is not an issue in Baruch's questions. Rather, all of Baruch's questions are variations on one major question: has God nullified the covenants He made with Abraham and Moses?[27]

In contrast, Ezra's basic premise is that the propensity to sin resulting from the evil heart makes it impossible for almost anyone to fulfill the Torah and thereby to obtain life. The sins which prompted God to deliver His city to the enemy are the last in a long string of examples of the effects of the evil heart (3:19-26; 7:116-20). Thus, Ezra's question is actually an accusation: God places demands on His people which they cannot fulfill, and then punishes them for their failure to do so. In addition, Ezra protests that God humiliates His people further by allowing nations more wicked than they to punish them (3:27-36).

(3) Uriel's responses to Ezra's grief also are addressed to questions different from those discussed by God and Baruch. The distinction between the *many* and the *few* occurs in the conversations between God and Baruch and in Uriel's words. In 2 Baruch, the distinction is used to identify as Israel the *few* Jews who have remained loyal to the Mosaic heritage, in contrast to the *many* Jews who have chosen the darkness of

---

[27]Similarly, Baruch is not addressing the question of whether the will is free in his later comments about the effects of Adam's sin on his descendants (48:42-47; 54:15, 19). Rather, he is expressing his consolation; because of the revelations he has received about the future, he can acknowledge God's justice and power in the present times.

Adam. The question of whether the human will is free is not a part of the discussion.

In contrast, Uriel uses the distinction to defend God's decision to let the *many* sinners perish, while the *few* righteous persons obtain salvation (7:11-14, 20-25, 70-73; 7:127-8:3). Here the distinction is part of the argument about theodicy; Uriel is arguing that the structure of creation does not deprive the individual of his ability to attain salvation. Central to Uriel's argument is the assertion, contra Ezra, that the individual is completely free to make his/her decision vis-à-vis God.

(4) Although Ezra and Baruch both move to consolation because of the revelations they receive about the future, the nature of those revelations differs significantly. Baruch converses with God, and gains knowledge about the future which enables him to acknowledge that his grief has been resolved. Moreover, repeatedly he shares the revelation he has received with his community.

In contrast, Ezra sees the heavenly city (10:25-55) and he receives two visions of the end-time, which are interpreted for him (11:1-12:34; 13:1-52). Although obviously he is consoled, Ezra never explicitly acknowledges that his accusations have been refuted. Moreover, much of the revelation he has received is for the exclusive use of the wise within his community (12:35-39; 14:44-48).

(5) The relationship of Baruch and Ezra to their respective communities illustrates yet another difference between the agendas of the two books. Baruch is a pastoral figure to all his people; he shares with them the revelations he has received, transfers the leadership from himself to others when his death approaches, and reassures the people that their continued survival is guaranteed because of the Torah and the leaders it will spawn. Moreover, his community's response to him plays an important role in the unfolding of the story. Baruch's final legacy to his people is the book which bears his name.

In contrast, Ezra has very little contact with his people, and he offers only superficial responses to their fears that he is abandoning them (6:16-19; 12:40-49). Moreover, Ezra learns that there is a distinction within his community between the *wise* and the *many*. He is told to withhold certain esoteric knowledge from the general public and to transmit it only to the few *wise* persons who can understand it. Consequently, he leaves two legacies—the Torah for the general public, and other books for the exclusive use of the *wise* among his people.

The contrasts between the encounters of Baruch and Ezra with their communities provide a particularly interesting insight into the literary structures of the two books. Baruch's three encounters with his community are essential to the story which is being told. Ezra also meets with his people or their leader three times (5:16-19; 12:40-49; 14:27-36). In the first two meetings, the people or their leader express a feeling of abandonment similar to that expressed by Baruch's community. In the final encounter, Ezra delivers a speech to all the people which bears little, if any, relationship to the revelations he has received throughout the book. Interestingly, none of the three encounters is an essential component in the development of the book; if they were omitted, their absence hardly would be noticed.[28] Thus, at least in this respect, the literary structure of 4 Ezra lacks the cohesiveness of the structure of 2 Baruch.

In addition to the different agendas of the two books, there are at least two ways in which the response of 4 Ezra to the events of 70 C.E. develops in directions far removed from the response of 2 Baruch. These directions are discussed by W. Harnisch and G. Scholem.

In his analysis of the relationship between fate and the promise in 4 Ezra, Harnisch observes that there are statements in 4 Ezra which are not far removed from a gnostic position.[29] Although it does not reflect a gnostic stance, 4 Ezra's emphasis on esoteric knowledge attainable only by a few wise persons parallels a characteristic of gnostic writings, where such knowledge results in salvation. When considered together with the statement that creation itself is under judgment (7:11), Ezra's deprecation of human ability could easily develop into the negative view of life in this world which also is characteristic of gnosticism.[30] R. M. Grant has suggested that the failure of Jewish apocalyptic thought was one factor contributing to the development of gnosticism.[31] Although 4 Ezra certainly is not a gnostic document, there are clues that the author was

---

[28]In fact, this is what scholars tend to do. The encounters between Ezra and his people are mentioned only rarely in analyses of 4 Ezra. E. Breech ("These Fragments," 271-74) includes the encounters as part of his evidence that each episode ends with a narrative segment which moves the action forward. However, he does not differentiate between the encounters and other concluding narrative phrases, and he does not seem particularly interested in the dynamics at work in each encounter.

[29]Harnisch, *Verhängnis*, 49-72.

[30]For a general discussion of gnosticism, see H. Jonas, *The Gnostic Religion: The Message of the Alien God and the Beginning of Christianity* (2d ed.; Boston: Beacon Press, 1963).

[31]R. M. Grant, *Gnosticism and Early Christianity* (2d ed.; New York: Columbia University Press, 1966) 27-38.

dealing with a situation in which the evolution of elements of apocalyptic thought into a gnostic position was a distinct possibility.

G. Scholem situates 4 Ezra within a different context—the development of various forms of apocalyptic literature into merkabah mysticism.[32]   Scholem does not argue that 4 Ezra is an example of mystical literature; however, he identifies motifs within the book which seem to indicate a development in the direction of mystical thought. Scholem's description of the characteristics of merkabah mysticism includes a number of motifs found in 4 Ezra: revelation through the voice "like the sound of rushing waters" (6:17); the emphasis on secret revelation which only the wise can understand (12:38; 14:46-47); the seven stages of joy through which the righteous dead enter into rest (7:90-98); the entrance into the heavenly city (10:55);[33] and the inspiration which enables Ezra to dictate the ninety-four books and the use of scribes to write his dictation (14:38-44). Scholem further notes the close association between various forms of merkabah mysticism and speculative gnosticizing tendencies.

In summary, the contributions of Harnisch and Scholem suggest that certain motifs in 4 Ezra quite possibly represent a preliminary step in the development of apocalyptic literature in a mystical—and perhaps somewhat gnostic—direction. 2 Baruch and 4 Ezra both tell a story in response to the events of 70 C.E. However, while Baruch's new knowledge of the future enables him and his entire community to face life in the present world with confidence, the secret revelation which Ezra receives and communicates to the wise enables them to enjoy a type of consolation not available to the rest of the community.

THE *APOCALYPSE OF ABRAHAM* AND 2 BARUCH

Introduction

The *Apocalypse of Abraham* is the account of Abraham's conversion from idolatry (chaps. 1-8) and of the revelations he receives after

---

[32]G. Scholem, *Major Trends in Jewish Mysticism* (New York: Schocken Books, 1974 reprint) 40-79.

[33]Usually, the mystics were taken to the divine throne. Thus, Ezra's experience is not exactly parallel at this point. See Scholem, *Major Trends*, 40-79.

ascending to the divine throne (chaps. 9-32).[34]   The destruction of the
Temple is included in these revelations (chap. 27).

The exact date of composition of the book is unknown. The terminus a quo is the destruction of Jerusalem in 70 C.E. Most scholars set the
upper limit of the time of composition near the end of the first century
C.E. or early in the second century C.E.[35]

Analysis

The biblical basis of the *Apocalypse of Abraham* is Genesis 15:6-21.
In the biblical text, Abraham offers a sacrifice as instructed by God and is
promised that his descendants will inherit the land.

In the *Apocalypse of Abraham,* the account of this sacrifice is
transformed into the mystical ascent of Abraham to the divine throne,
where he receives revelation.[36] The issues being addressed in this adaptation of the biblical model are apparent in the material which precedes
the ascent and in the revelations Abraham receives during and after the
ascent.

One of these issues is cultic defilement, construed as some sort of
idolatry. The *Apocalypse of Abraham* begins with the legend of Abraham's rejection of idolatry (chaps. 1-8). Because he abandons the idols of
his father Terah, Abraham is deemed worthy to see the future times. He
is instructed to purify himself forty days, and then to prepare the sacrifice. The function of this legend becomes clear after Abraham has
ascended to the divine throne and sees a vision of Solomon's Temple:

> I saw there [i.e., in the earthly Temple] the likeness of the
> idol of jealousy, having the likeness of woodwork such as my
> father used to make, and its statue was of glittering bronze;
> and before it a man, and he worshipped it; and in front of him
> an altar, and upon it a boy slain in the presence of altar . . .
> [God said] the statue which you saw is my anger wherewith

---

[34]See Nickelsburg (*Jewish Literature,* 294-99) for a helpful introduction to the text and its background. The primary translation and commentary on the text is that of G. H. Box, *The Apocalypse of Abraham*
(London: SPCK, 1919). The quotations from the *Apocalypse* are taken
from Box's translation, with a few modifications in style.

[35]Nickelsburg, *Jewish Literature,* 298-99; Box, *The Apocalypse,* xv-
xvi.

[36]The similarities between themes in the *Apocalypse of Abraham*
and merkabah mysticism are discussed by Scholem, *Major Trends,* 40-75.

the people anger Me who are to proceed from you. But the
man you saw slaughtering—--that is he who incites murderous
sacrifices. (chap. 25)[37]

The Temple cult is profaned by idolatrous practices. In contrast to Abraham's decision to abandon idolatry and follow God, his descendants have
chosen to use God's Temple as the setting for their idolatry. Two facets
of one question are implied in the discussion of the defiled cult: What will
happen to these Jews who take part in these idolatrous practices, and
what will happen to those Jews who have followed Abraham's example?

The second issue with which the book is concerned is the presence
and function of evil in the world, particularly with reference to the
oppression of Israel by the nations. This issue is introduced as Abraham
prepares to offer his sacrifice and is confronted by Azazel (chap. 13).
Azazel is the personification of evil: he has been given power by God
over all those who will to do evil (chaps. 13-14, 23-24). When he tries to
dissuade Abraham from making the sacrifice, the angel Yahoel tells him:

> Disgrace on you, Azazel! For Abraham's lot is in heaven, but
> yours is upon the earth. Because you have chosen and love
> this for the dwelling of your uncleanness, therefore the
> eternal mighty Lord made you a dweller on the earth and
> through you every evil spirit of lies, and through you wrath
> and trials for the generations of ungodly men; for God . . . has
> not permitted the bodies of the righteous to be in your hand,
> in order that thereby the life of the righteous and the
> destruction of the unclean may be assured. (chap. 13)

Thus, the righteous belong to God and the unrighteous to Azazel. Azazel's
power over the unclean guarantees their destruction.

After he has completed his sacrifice, Abraham ascends on the
wings of a pigeon through the heavens until finally he reaches the divine
throne (chaps. 15-18). God's subsequent conversation with him (chaps. 19-
32) develops further the question of evil, and resolves all of his questions
by reference to the final judgment.

God's statements to Abraham expand the question about the destinies of the righteous and the wicked to include the oppression of Israel by

---

[37] Based on biblical references, the "man who incites child sacrifices" almost certainly is King Manasseh. See 2 Kgs 21:1-18; 2 Chr 33:1-
20.

the nations. Abraham learns that Azazel has been given power over those who will to do evil (chap. 23); the decision to do evil, moreover, is a matter of free choice (chap. 26). It is at this point that Abraham sees the heavenly and earthly Temples, and finds out that the destruction of the Temple will be God's response to His people's idolatry (chap. 27).

In response to Abraham's question regarding how long the nations will oppress Israel, God describes the parts of time and the eschatological judgment (chaps. 28-29). He promises Abraham that his descendants will judge the lawless Gentiles. After ten plagues have covered the world, the righteous Jews will come to the Temple, offer sacrifices and gifts in the new age, and punish those who have oppressed them.

After this revelation, Abraham returns to earth and continues to converse with God (chaps. 30-32). Once again, the eschatological tableau is discussed. After reassuring Abraham that the Gentiles will be justly punished, God concludes by describing the final destinies of the Jews who have participated in the idolatrous practices:

> And I will give those who have covered Me with mockery to
> the scorn of the coming Age; and I have prepared them to be
> food for the fire of Hades and for ceaseless flight to and fro
> through the air in the underworld beneath the earth,[38] the
> body filled with worms. For on them shall they see the
> righteous of the Creator—those, namely, who have chosen to
> do My will, and those who have openly kept My command-
> ments, and they shall rejoice with joy over the downfall of
> the men who still remain, who have followed the idols and
> their murders. For they shall putrefy in the body of the evil
> worm Azazel, and be burned with the fire of Azazel's tongue;
> for I hoped that they would come to me, and not have loved
> and praised the strange [god], and not have adhered to him for
> whom they were not allotted, but they have forsaken the
> Mighty Lord. (chap. 32)

Comparison with 2 Baruch

At first glance, the *Apocalypse of Abraham* and 2 Baruch appear to be extremely dissimilar documents. However, a close examination indi- cates that they are linked to each other by a series of common traditions.

---

[38]There is a manuscript problem here. The oldest manuscript of the text (Codex Sylvester) stops at this point. However, two Palaea versions of the book contain the final verses. See Box, *Apocalypse,* xiii-xiv.

The key to these traditions is the use of Abrahamic imagery in each book. At least three series of common traditions can be identified on the basis of this imagery.

(1) In both books, the destruction calls into question the efficacy of the covenant God made with Abraham. In 2 Baruch, this question is formulated in terms of the loss of the land God promised to Abraham's descendants forever. In the *Apocalypse of Abraham,* this question is formulated primarily in terms of the continued oppression of Abraham's descendants by the nations. As in 2 Baruch, the survival of Israel is perceived to be at stake. Both books assert that the covenant has not been nullified; at the eschaton it will be apparent to all that God keeps His promises to His faithful people.

(2) In both books, there is a connection between the figure of Abraham, the conviction that the cult in Jerusalem was defiled prior to the destruction, and the figure of Manasseh. In 2 Baruch, the typology between Baruch/Abraham introduces a typology between Jerusalem/ Sodom (see above, Excursus A). Implied in the second typology is the conviction that Jerusalem, like Sodom before it, was an extremely sinful city. This motif is explicated in two places: the conversation between God and Baruch (4G—chaps. 41-43) which deals with the transgressions of the *many* Jews who forfeited the covenant relationship by assimilation to the ways of the nations; and in the legend of Manasseh recorded in the interpretation of the cloud/waters vision (chaps. 64-65). Manasseh functions as a prototype of the *many* Jews; his sins are described as involving cultic abuses, including the building of an idol. Because he is the prototype of these Jews, we can infer that their sins probably included cultic violations.

In the *Apocalypse of Abraham,* it is precisely Abraham's rejection of idolatry which motivates God to reveal Himself to him, and it is the practice of idolatry by Abraham's descendants which motivates God to allow the destruction of Jerusalem. Moreover, the cultic abuses of Manasseh are described as the primary example of the cultic defilement (chap. 25). Thus here, as in 2 Baruch, the figure of Abraham, the indictment of the cult, and the figure of Manasseh are all interrelated.

(3) Both books refer to the ascent of Abraham to the heavenly world. The ascent is mentioned in 2 Baruch in God's comments about the heavenly Temple (1B—4:4). It is the essential element in the literary structure of the *Apocalypse.*

In addition to the evidence of similar traditions in the *Apocalypse of Abraham* and 2 Baruch, there also are some significant differences between the books. The *Apocalypse of Abraham* lacks the emphasis on the Torah and its teachers which is essential to 2 Baruch's assurance that "Israel" will survive in this world. Moreover, the narrative worlds of the two books are completely different. The author of the *Apocalypse* elaborates the biblical story of Abraham's sacrifice (Genesis 15:6-21) into a mystical ascent in which the patriarch is given a preview of how his descendants will sin and be punished, and how the nations and the righteous and wicked within Israel will fare at the eschatological judgment. The personification of evil in the figure of Azazel also distinguishes the *Apocalypse of Abraham* from 2 Baruch. Here the *Apocalypse* is much closer to the "evil heart" imagery of 4 Ezra.

THE *PARALEIPOMENA OF JEREMIAH* AND 2 BARUCH

Introduction

The *Paraleipomena of Jeremiah* or *The Things Omitted from Jeremiah*, is a narrative account of the destruction of Jerusalem (chaps. 1-4) and of the return of the exiles sixty-six years later (chaps. 5-9).[39] In its present form, the book is a mixed Jewish/Christian composition. The evidence suggests that the present text probably is a Christian redaction of an original Jewish work.[40]

The exact date of composition of the *Paraleipomena of Jeremiah* is unknown. However, the sixty-six year interval between the destruction and the return suggests that the book was composed ca. 136 C.E. This date coincides with the Second Revolt and the decree of Hadrian that no Jews be allowed to enter Jerusalem.[41]

---

[39]For a concise introduction to the book, see Nickelsburg, *Jewish Literature*, 313-16. See also M. Stone, "Baruch, Rest of Words of," *EncJud* 4. 270-71. The primary translation of the text is: R. Kraft and A Purintun, ed. and trans., *Paraleipomena Jeremiou* (SBLTT 1, Ps Ser.1; Missoula: SBL, 1972).

[40]Stone, "Baruch, Rest of . . . ," 270-71. As support for the thesis of a Jewish original, Stone lists what he perceives to be the dominant Jewish features of the book: the approval of sacrifice, the rejection of foreign women, and the attitude toward circumcision. The various hypotheses regarding the original composition of the book can be reduced to three: it was written by a Jewish Christian for a Jewish-Christian audience; it represents the Church's eirenicon to the Jewish community; or it was a Jewish document into which Christian material later was inserted. See Kraft, *Paraleipomenou*, 8-10.

[41]Nickelsburg, *Jewish Literature*, 315-16.

Analysis

The *Paraleipomena of Jeremiah* begins with a narrative account of the days immediately prior to the destruction of Jerusalem by Babylon (chaps. 1-4). God tells Jeremiah that He will destroy the city because of the people's sins, and He instructs him to leave the city with Baruch.[42] Jeremiah requests that God overthrow the city Himself lest the enemy boast, and God agrees to do so.[43] Later, Jeremiah and Baruch see the angels coming with torches. At Jeremiah's request, God allows him to bury the Temple vessels so that they will be safe until "the gathering of the beloved" (3:8-11).[44] Also at Jeremiah's request, God agrees that Abimilech will be preserved from the destruction. He tells Jeremiah to send him to the vineyard of Agrippa (3:12-22). After the destruction, Jeremiah is taken captive to Babylon, while Baruch remains in the city and laments what has happened. Even in his lament, he expresses confidence that the enemy will be destroyed and the exiles will return home. (4:7-10).[45]

The action continues sixty-six years later, when Abimilech awakes from the sleep which God had caused to fall upon him (chap. 5). Taking with him his figs, which remained ripe the entire time, Abimilech goes to Baruch. Baruch is still sitting on the tomb to which he retired after his lament sixty-six years earlier (6:1-2). He interprets the miracle of the figs as a sign of the resurrection of the body and as an indication that the time has come for the exiles to return home (6:3-11). In response to Baruch's prayer (6:12-14), an angel tells him to write to Jeremiah that, after fifteen days, those Jews who separate themselves from Babylon can return home (6:15-25). Baruch sends the message by eagle to Babylon (7:1-22).

Jeremiah writes a reply to Baruch, which emphasizes the sufferings of the exiles (7:24-36).[46] He then spends the remainder of the time prior to the departure exhorting the people to abstain from the pollutions of the Gentiles (7:37). At God's command, Jeremiah leads the people from Babylon to the Jordan River. There he announces that mixed marriages

---

[42]Cf. 2 Baruch chaps. 1-2.

[43]Cf. 2 Baruch 5:1-3.

[44]Cf. 2 Baruch chaps. 6-8.

[45]Cf. 2 Baruch 10:6-11:7. In 2 Baruch, Baruch's lament does not include a statement of confidence that the exiles will return home.

[46]In their anguish, the people even were praying to foreign gods (7:29).

must be dissolved (chap. 8). The Jews who meet the requirements return to Jerusalem (9:1). Soon thereafter, Jeremiah dies (9:7-32).[47]

Comparison with 2 Baruch

The destruction of Jerusalem in 587 B.C.E. provides the biblical basis for 2 Baruch and the *Paraleipomena of Jeremiah*. Verbal similarities between the early parts of both books quite possibly indicate that the authors are adapting a common tradition about the destruction.[48] However, the agendas of the two books are quite different.

The primary difference between the two books was discussed in Chapter IV: the *Paraleipomena of Jeremiah* declares that return is imminent, while 2 Baruch argues that it is not.[49] The author of 2 Baruch reshapes the Jeremianic tradition that the exiles would return after seventy years (Jeremiah 29:7-14) and announces that the restoration will occur at the eschaton. In contrast, the author of the *Paraleipomena of Jeremiah* uses the literary device of a sixty-six year time period to indicate that the return will occur in his own time; if the exiles purify themselves of foreign practices and marriages, they will return home soon.

There also are several other differences between the books. The relationship of Baruch to Jeremiah is reversed in the two books. Moreover, while the *Paraleipomena of Jeremiah* portrays Jeremiah as the leader of the community, it does not discuss the issue of who will succeed him in this capacity. Moreover, while it stresses the importance of abolishing mixed marriages in preparation for the return, the *Paraleipomena of Jeremiah* does not emphasize that the Torah is the basis of the community's continued existence. The efficacy of God's justice and power are not question in this book.

---

[47] The book concludes (chap. 9) with two accounts of the death of Jeremiah. The influence of a Christian redactor or author is obvious in this chapter.

[48] G. Nickelsburg, "Narrative Traditions in the *Paraleipomena of Jeremiah* and 2 Baruch," *CBQ* 35 (1973) 60-68. Nickelsburg argues convincingly, contra Bogaert, that the *Paraleipomena of Jeremiah* and 2 Baruch reflect adaptations of a common source rather than the dependence of one book upon the other. The basis of Nickelsburg's argument is the presence in both books of elements of a primitive tradition also attested in 2 Maccabees.

[49] See above, p. 113.

THE GOSPEL OF MATTHEW AND 2 BARUCH

Introduction

The Gospel of Matthew is a Christian document composed near the end of the first century C.E.[50] It is included here because it deals with some of the same kinds of issues as does 2 Baruch. The two books will be compared on the basis of four themes: (1) the significance of the destruction of the Temple; (2) the status of Jews and Gentiles; (3) the basis of the community's continued existence; and (4) the grounds of eschatological expectation.

Analysis

Matthew is an account of the life of Jesus, which discusses his identity, teachings, and fate, and describes the communication of his legacy to his community. Throughout Matthew, the identity of Jesus is described in terms of the fulfillment of scriptural prophecies.[51] In this way, he and his work are construed as the goal of the prophetic message.[52] At the same time, Jesus also is portrayed as Wisdom incarnate.[53]

Jesus' teaching emphasizes that in his person the Kingdom of Heaven is at hand. Physical descent from Abraham is no longer a decisive factor; a person's relationship to the Father is determined by his attitude toward Jesus (e.g., 3:7-12; 8:10-12). According to Matthew, Jesus does not abrogate the Torah; on the contrary, he fulfills it by interpreting it correctly (e.g., 5:1-7:29; 12:1-7).[54] The love of God and the doing of His

---

[50]W. G. Kümmel, *Introduction to the New Testament* (14th rev. ed.; New York: Abingdon Press, 1966) 84.

[51]E.g., 1:23; 2:6, 23; 4:15-16; 8:17; 12:17-21; 13:35; 21:4-5; 26:56.

[52]D. Hare (*The Theme of Jewish Persecution of Christians in the Gospel of Matthew* [Cambridge: Harvard University Press, 1967] 159-60) notes that the use of Old Testament prophecies in this way enables the author to use Christology as the connecting link between the "old" and the "new" periods of salvation history.

[53]M. J. Suggs, *Wisdom, Christology, and Law in Matthew's Gospel* (Cambridge: Harvard University Press, 1970) 58-61, 99-128. Suggs argues convincingly that the revision of older Wisdom sayings in Matt 11:28-30 and 23:34-37 illustrates the way in which Jesus is identified as Wisdom incarnate by the author of Matthew.

[54]See also 15:1-9; 19:3-9; 22:15-46; 23:1-36. Hare (*The Theme*, 141-

will to others remains the criterion by which a person will be judged at the final judgment. Moreover, all moral action has a Christological function; a person's service to his fellow man is at the same time service to Jesus the Lord (e.g., 7:21; 19:16-22; 25:31-46).

Throughout Matthew, Jesus asserts that the Kingdom is present in him, and he claims to offer the authoritative interpretation of the Torah. This leads to increasing conflict with the Jewish religious leaders (e.g. 12:1-4, 22-45; 15:1-9).[55] Their refusal to accept Jesus' message results in a gradual shift to the Gentiles as the focus of Jesus' ministry (e.g., 9:1-13; 15:21-28; 20:1-16; 21:28-22:14).[56]

The destruction of the Temple is mentioned within Jesus' final denunciation of the Jewish leaders (23:29-39). After rebuking the scribes and Pharisees for their hypocrisy (23:1-28), Jesus exhorts them to complete their fathers' work of murdering the prophets. Their punishment is at hand; the destruction of the Temple will be a visible sign of God's rejection of them.[57] Moreover, there are indications that Matthew believes that the Temple cult itself was defiled. The day after Jesus has entered Jerusalem and cleansed the Temple (21:12-13), he returns to the Temple and encounters the chief priests and elders of the people. He directs the parables of the two sons and of the vineyard to them, telling them that the kingdom will be taken away from them (21:23-43). Implied

---

43) correctly observes that the abrogation of the Torah is not the issue in Jesus' conflict with the Jewish leaders. The crux of the issue is Jesus' interpretation of the Torah. Cf. Suggs, *Wisdom*, 99-128; W. D. Davies, *The Sermon on the Mount* (Cambridge: Harvard University Press, 1966) 84-90.

[55]Cf. 16:5-12; 19:3-9; 21:14-16, 23-27. In addition, see S. van Tilborg, *Jewish Leaders in Matthew* (Leiden: E. J. Brill, 1972), 168-72.

[56]This transition is foreshadowed in 2:7-12. The Jewish king Herod seeks to kill the baby Jesus, while the Gentile wisemen seek to worship him. The initial commissioning of the disciples to go throughout Israel and abstain from contact with the Gentiles (chap. 10) suggests that originally Jesus' mission was perceived to be directed solely to Israel.

[57]Cf. the preceding parable (22:1-14), where the angry King (i.e., God) sends troops to "kill those murderers (i.e., Jews) and set their city (i.e., Jerusalem) on fire" (22:7). Hare (*The Theme*, 131, 151-56) suggests that Matthew has developed an old Jewish tradition about Israel's rejection of the prophets into an established "law of history." Suggs (*Wisdom*, 58-61) agrees that the destruction is a sign of Israel's punishment. However, his model is the ongoing rejection of Wisdom's envoys.

in the parables is the conviction that these cultic figures have failed in their responsibilities to the "owner of the vineyard."[58]

Jesus' fate is death in Jerusalem, after "suffering many things from the elders, chief priests, and scribes" (16:21; 20:17-19; 26:54).[59] The Jews are portrayed as the villains in the crucifixion; by continuing their ancestral pattern of killing the prophets, they make themselves responsible for the death of God's final messenger to them (23:29-37; 26:3ff.; 28:1ff.).[60] Because they reject Jesus, God rejects them as His people. The status and prerogatives of Israel are transferred to the community of Jesus' followers, which is described by Jesus as "my church" (16:18).[61]

According to Matthew, Jesus' death is followed by his resurrection three days later and his appearances to the women and the disciples (chap. 28). His final words to his community include instructions and a promise. The disciples are instructed to make disciples of the nations by baptizing them and teaching them to observe what Jesus has commanded. They are promised that the risen Jesus, now possessing all authority on heaven and earth, will remain among them until the close of the age.

As recipients of the risen Jesus' commission, the disciples assume a position of leadership within the community. The actual conferral of leadership is recorded earlier in 16:13-20. After Peter has identified Jesus as the Christ, the Son of the living God, he is told "on this rock I will build my Church, and the powers of death will not prevail against it" (16:18). The Church is given the keys to the Kingdom of Heaven; as it binds and loosens on earth, so it will be done in heaven.[62]

---

[58] See G. Nickelsburg, "Enoch, Levi, and Peter: Recipients of Revelation in Upper Galilee," *JBL* 100/4 (1981) 575-600. He discusses evidence in Matthew of disenchantment with the Jerusalem priesthood, and he tentatively proposes that Peter is portrayed as a counterpart to, or replacement of, the Jewish high priest. Cf. 2 Baruch 10:18.

[59] Cf. 26:1-5, 59; 27:1ff.

[60] Matt 27:25 is especially important in this context. In response to Pilate's declaration that Jesus is innocent, "all the people" reply that Jesus' blood should be on them and their children.

[61] The permanent rejection of Israel and the transfer of the kingdom to the Gentiles is graphically described in the parables of the two sons, the vineyard tenants, and the marriage feast (21:28-22:14). See also W. Trilling, "Das Wahre Israel," *Studien Zum Alten und Neuen Testament* 10 (1964) 1-224; Hare, *The Theme,* 139, 151-60.

[62] G. Nickelsburg ("Enoch, Levi, and Peter," 594-95) observes that the loosening/binding imagery probably refers to the authority to exclude people from the community and to reinstate them.

Thus, according to Matthew, the possession of the Kingdom of Heaven passes to the new people of God. The Jews have lost the status of "Israel"; the true Israel which confesses that "Jesus is Lord" is commissioned to spread his message throughout the Gentile world.[63] The ongoing presence of the Risen Lord among his people guarantees the survival of the faithful community until the eschaton.

Comparison with 2 Baruch

Unlike 2 Baruch, Matthew does not use the destruction of 587 B.C.E. as a model for the destruction of 70 C.E. Instead, he elaborates Israel's past rejection of the prophets into an historical pattern of rejection which culminates in the death of Jesus, the last of God's messengers to Israel. On the basis of this pattern, Matthew interprets the destruction as a sign of Israel's punishment and of God's *permanent* rejection of her. Matthew's stated reason for God's rejection of the Jews is their refusal to accept Jesus as Messiah. Because they have rejected Jesus as the Messiah, their former status as "Israel" has been totally abrogated. The prerogatives and responsibilities of "Israel" have been transferred to the Christian community, which includes both Gentiles and Jews. The mission of the new "Israel" is directed primarily toward the Gentiles.

2 Baruch and Matthew share an interest in the survival of the faithful community, particularly in terms of ongoing leadership. In both books, the impending death of the main character necessitates a transition in leadership from him to his successors. According to Matthew, the risen Lord remains present among his community to guide and help them; in 2 Baruch, the Torah has basically the same function.

Matthew and 2 Baruch also share the conviction that history is moving toward its conclusion, and that the Torah will be the criterion which determines the individual's eschatological destiny. The indissoluble connection between Torah and the return of Jesus as judge (Mattew 25:31-

---

[63] According to Matthew, the true Israel includes Jews and Gentiles who confess that Jesus is Lord. Within the author's own community, the transition from almost an exclusive Jewish-Christian constituency to a Gentile composition seems to have been gradual and somewhat painful. Scholars continue to debate whether the split between Church and synagogue was completed when Matthew was composed. See J. Rohde, *Rediscovering the Teachings of the Evangelists* (London: SCM Press, 1968) 25-29; D. Harrington, "Matthean Studies Since Joachin Rohde," *HeyJ* 16 (1975) 375-88.

46) distinguishes the eschatological expectation of Matthew from that of 2 Baruch.

In summary, Matthew and 2 Baruch deal with many of the same kinds of issues. However, Matthew's conviction that Jesus is Messiah establishes an unbridgeable gap between the two books: when the old traditions are reevaluated in the light of this new conviction, there is no room for the message of 2 Baruch. G. Nickelsburg reiterates this point:

> In these contrasting hopes and differing appraisals of the year 70 we see the dividing of the ways: the tragic splitting of Christianity from Judaism, the children leaving one Mother for another.[64]

CONCLUSION

In an article entitled "Judaism in a Time of Crisis: Four Responses to the Destruction of the Second Temple," Jacob Neusner examines the impact of the events of 70 C.E. on four groups of people: apocalyptic writers, the Dead Sea sect, the Christian Church, and the Pharisees.[65] On the basis of 4 Ezra and what he terms "The Vision of Baruch,"[66] Neusner describes the apocalyptic response to the events of 70 C.E. as follows:

> When the apocalyptic visionaries looked backward upon the ruins, they saw a tragic vision. So they emphasized the future, supernatural redemption, which they believed was soon to come. . . . *The response of the visionaries* is, thus, *essentially negative.* All they had to say is that God is just and Israel has sinned, but, in the end of time, there will be redemption. What to do *in the meantime*? Merely wait. Not much of an answer. (emphasis added)[67]

---

[64]Nickelsburg, *Jewish Literature,* 305.

[65]J. Neusner, "Judaism in a Time of Crisis: Four Responses to the Destruction of the Second Temple," *Judaism* 21/3 (1972) 313-27. The article is reprinted in J. Neusner, *Early Rabbinic Judaism* (E. J. Brill, 1975) 34-49.

[66]Neusner includes the apocryphal Baruch and 2 Baruch in "The Vision of Baruch." He does not note the differences between the messages of the books (see above, p. 113). He also does not observe that 1 Baruch was written at least one hundred years before the common era. He treats the two books together, as if they were parts of one similar response to destruction and dispersion.

[67]Ibid., 315, 317.

Our comparison of 2 Baruch with related documents requires that we refine this assertion. There is no such thing as "the response of the visionaries"; there were a variety of responses, formulated in different ways. Moreover, far from being "essentially negative," the various Jewish responses emphasize the conviction that God has not abandoned His people; He will guide them in this world, as well as giving them life in the future world. There are many tasks to complete "in the meantime" prior to the consummation: there are communities to reconstruct and lead, and there are revelations to learn and to communicate to succeeding generations.

Nonetheless, although the phrase "the response of the visionaries" underestimates the diversity in these documents, it is true that the books reflect common traditions and are responding to a common question. The common traditions are, for the most part, no longer extant in their entirety. Their contours, however, can be identified on the basis of thematic and terminological similarities between the materials appearing in various forms in different documents. Several examples of these common traditions can be summarized briefly.

(1) The reference to Abraham's mystical experience in 2 Baruch 4:4 suggests that the author was aware of the mystical tradition about Abraham which appears in the *Apocalypse of Abraham*. A possible reference to this tradition also is recorded in 4 Ezra 3:13-14. It is not mentioned in the *Paraleipomena of Jeremiah* or in Pseudo-Philo. (2) The terminological and thematic similarities between 2 Baruch and 4 Ezra indicate that the authors probably had a source of common traditional material which dealt with the effects on mankind of Adam's sin. This theme reappears in the *Apocalypse of Abraham* 23 and in *3 Baruch* 4:8-17. It is rather conspicuously absent from Pseudo-Philo's retelling of biblical history, and it also does not occur in the *Paraleipomena of Jeremiah*. (3) Terminological similarities between the *Paraleipomena of Jeremiah* and the early parts of 2 Baruch (i.e., chaps. 1-11) indicate the presence of a common Jeremianic tradition about the destruction of 587 B.C.E. Interestingly, this tradition does not occur in the other documents included in this study. (4) All of the documents anticipate some kind of eschatological restoration. The common conviction that history is moving toward the eschaton unites the diverse traditions used, even within any one document, to express this eschatological hope.

There is a common denominator in the utilization of all these traditions by the various authors. That denominator is the question of the survival of Israel in the face of her oppression and defeat by the nations.

The way in which each author formulates and resolves this question accounts for the diversity in these responses to the events of 70 C.E.

Pseudo-Philo and 2 Baruch both formulate this question in terms of God's fidelity to the covenant relationship, and both emphasize the role of the Torah and ongoing leadership in the maintenance of that relationship. However, the type of leadership envisioned in Pseudo-Philo is more diverse than in 2 Baruch. The *Apocalypse of Abraham* shares the emphasis on the covenant, but does not deal with the issue of leadership. Moreover, unlike Pseudo-Philo, the *Apocalypse of Abraham* and 2 Baruch use the discussion about the covenant as a format from which to express the conviction that the Temple cult was defiled prior to the destruction.

4 Ezra also probes the relationship of the destruction to God's covenantal promises to His people. However, his reflections and speculations lead to accusations against God based on the way in which He has structured all of creation. By asserting that man's created propensity to sin makes it impossible for almost anyone to obtain salvation, Ezra moves the discussion about the efficacy of God's promises in a different direction than that taken by the other documents. Also unique to 4 Ezra is the contrast between the *wise* and the *many*. The motif of esoteric knowledge understandable only by the wise elite within the community is alien to the other documents.

The *Paraleipomena of Jeremiah* bypasses the questions and uses a narrative story to give the answer. The author is convinced that restoration is imminent; all the people need do is prepare themselves for it. This sense of immediacy is lacking in the other documents.

In summary, there are both basic similarities and striking differences in the responses of these documents to the events of 70 C.E. The documents reveal that in the aftermath of the destruction the Jewish people were confronted by a massive theological problem. In general, these documents deal with the problem of the survival of Israel by attempting to justify the ways of God to man on theological grounds and by exhorting their readers to choose the alternative of faith in God's promises. The diversity in the documents is due to the various ways in which the answers to the problem are formulated. This diversity highlights the uniqueness of 2 Baruch as a theological document and gives us clues to the situation in Palestine near the end of the first century C.E.

The author of 2 Baruch takes a very practical approach to the theological problem. He acknowledges the reasons for the destruction, expresses the grief which followed it, and systematically works through the issues precipitated by it. He assures his readers that faith is possible for them because of their knowledge of the eschatological future and of their historical past. His theological reflections are integrated with his practical concern—the reconstitution of the faithful community for continued life in this world and time. In this practical approach to life in this world, we see a point of similarity between 2 Baruch and later rabbinic Judaism.

In contrast, the author of 4 Ezra takes a much more speculative approach to the theological problem. He uses the particular example of the destruction to probe the universal implications of the way in which all creation is structured. His theological speculations culminate in a resolution to the problem through a "leap of faith." In the conversations between Uriel and Ezra and in Ezra's activities, we see glimpses of motifs which are not far removed from the worlds of merkabah mysticism and gnostic speculation.

Because there is a special literary relationship between 2 Baruch and 4 Ezra, the contrasts between the books are particularly helpful in highlighting the uniqueness of 2 Baruch. Unlike the author of 4 Ezra, the author of 2 Baruch does not use his traditional material as the basis for anthropological speculation. He simply is not interested in the implications of man's status as creature within God's creation. Rather, he applies his traditional material to the practical question of the reconstitution of the community which he perceives to be faithful "Israel." The contrast between the practical, pastoral thrust of 2 Baruch and the speculative interests of 4 Ezra helps to explain why scholars have tended to misconstrue 2 Baruch as a shallow step-sister of 4 Ezra. If 2 Baruch is approached as a speculative document, then it indeed appears to be a shallow, simplistic version of 4 Ezra. However, when it is approached as a document in its own right, its uniqueness becomes apparent. Then it can be appreciated as a compelling account of one author's effort to relate his theological reflections to the practical issue of the continued life of his community.

The author of the *Apocalypse of Abraham* arrives at basically the same theological conclusions as does the author of 2 Baruch. He does not, however, apply these conclusions to the practical needs of any community. Moreover, the vehicle of his answer is the ascent of Abraham through the heavens to the divine throne. Through the use of this literary device, the author expresses the conviction that faith is possible because of the knowledge gained through this journey. In the description of Abraham's ascent, we see motifs of merkabah mysticism. In the personification of evil in the figure of Azazel, we see glimpses of the cosmic dualism between good and evil which is characteristic of gnostic writings.

The contrasts between the *Apocalypse of Abraham* and 2 Baruch illustrate the divergent ways in which commitment to the old covenantal traditions was being expressed in this time period. The author of 2 Baruch emphasizes the consolation available to the corporate community through knowledge of their eschatological future and their covenantal past, and through submission to the God of the covenant. The author of the *Apocalypse of Abraham* emphasizes the consolation available to the individual through the perspective on the covenant gained in the context of a journey through the heavenly world.

The author of Pseudo-Philo also arrives at basically the same theological conclusions as does the author of 2 Baruch. His conclusions, however, are based on the premise that God's actions in the past are an unchanging paradigm for His activity in the present and the future. In Pseudo-Philo, we see an example of one author's attempt to use a particular biblical pattern to explain the present and to strengthen the faith of a beleaguered community.

There are two particularly significant contrasts between 2 Baruch and Pseudo-Philo. 2 Baruch argues that knowledge of what God will do in the future makes it possible to live confidently in the present; Pseudo-Philo argues that knowledge of what God has done in the past makes it possible to live confidently in the present. The authors of Pseudo-Philo and 2 Baruch both deal with the question of ongoing leadership of the faithful community. The type of leadership envisioned in Pseudo-Philo is much broader than the model suggested in 2 Baruch. This difference highlights the way in which the author of 2 Baruch has defined leadership primarily in terms of interpretation of the Torah for the people.

The author of the *Paraleipomena of Jeremiah* bypasses the questions raised by the destruction. The book is an expression of faith that the return is imminent. The comparison of this narrative account with 2 Baruch illustrates how two authors have adapted a common narrative tradition to deliver messages which stand in tension with each other. From the *Paraleipomena of Jeremiah*, we learn that some Jews continued to expect that the return of ca 547 B.C.E. would be repeated ca. 136 C.E.

Finally, the Christian Gospel of Matthew illustrates how the question and the answers underwent a major transformation when the central datum became the conviction that Jesus is the Messiah. Faith is defined as trust in Jesus. In the light of this conviction, Matthew declares that the Jews who have not accepted Jesus as Messiah have been permanently rejected by God. From his perspective, God remains loyal to His covenantal commitment; however, the "Israel" to whom the covenant applies is the Christian community. The defeat of the "old" Israel by the nations is only a sign that the covenantal relationship between God and the Jewish people has been severed completely.

The comparison of all these documents with 2 Baruch highlights the theological uniqueness of 2 Baruch. This document lacks speculation, cosmic dualism, and mystical themes. It views the past and the present through the lens of the future, and on this basis it develops a practical response to the events of 70 C.E. This response is directed to the whole community; it is neither the property of the wise elite nor the possession simply of the righteous individual.

The comparison also enables us to make a few generalizations about the situation in Palestine ca. 100 C.E.[68] We have seen that the destruction precipitated a profound theological crisis among the Jewish people. The authors considered in this chapter utilized the Scriptures and other common traditions in order to make a response of faith in the midst of chaos. The variety of ways in which these affirmations of faith are developed accounts for the diversity of responses within what Neusner calls "the apocalyptic response" to the events of 70 C.E.

------

[68]I do not mean to imply that all of these documents necessarily were written in Palestine. Rather, they are responses to what was happening in Palestine during this time period.

VI

Conclusion

SUMMARY

In this dissertation, I have examined 2 Baruch as an integrated literary whole and have attempted to draw out of its parts the message of the document. I have discussed what we can learn from 2 Baruch about the real world of its author. I have also compared 2 Baruch with a number of related documents in order to highlight the literary and theological uniqueness of 2 Baruch and to acquire new evidence about the situation in Palestine near the end of the first century C.E.

In Chapter II, I analyzed the literary structure of the book. This analysis indicated that the author has structured his work in order to tell a story—a story in which Baruch and then his community move from grief to consolation. This story is carried by units of narrative prose, which incorporate non-narrative literary sub-units (e.g., laments, prayers, visions, conversations) into the narrative frame. By means of this story, the author develops the primary theological issues with which he is concerned. He does this by clustering the various sub-units and arranging them into seven blocks, in which he raises and then progressively resolves the issues with which he is concerned. The result is a coherent and artistically composed document, which moves smoothly from its beginning to its conclusion.

In Chapter III, I used my analysis of the literary structure of the book to examine in detail the primary theological issues which emerged in the course of the analysis. These issues are: the vindication of God's justice and power in the wake of the destruction of 70 C.E.; and the survival of the Jewish community in the aftermath of the destruction. I showed that both issues are parts of a single argument about theodicy. At stake is the continued efficacy of the covenant which God made with His people through Abraham and Moses. The exposition of these issues indicated that the blocks of material are related to each other in their content, terminology, and structure.

In Chapter IV, I discussed what we can learn from 2 Baruch about the real world of its author. After examining the history of research, I argued that the exact date of composition of the book is uncertain; all that we can say with certainty is that the terminus a quo for its writing is 70 C.E. Then I attempted to draw out of the text some clues to the author's perception of his real world.

In Chapter V, I compared 2 Baruch with four other Jewish responses to the events of 70 C.E. (Pseudo-Philo, 4 Ezra, the *Apocalypse of Abraham*, the *Paraleipomena of Jeremiah*) and with the Gospel of Matthew. The similarities and differences between these documents and 2 Baruch highlighted the uniqueness of 2 Baruch as a religious and theological document. In particular, the comparison underscored what we have seen in Chapters II-III—namely, 2 Baruch's practical concern with ongoing life in this world. On the other hand, the comparison also revealed that the various documents reflect common traditions and are responding to a common theological question. The various ways of answering this question reflect the diversity of ways in which teachers and leaders struggled with the theological crisis precipitated by the destruction of 70 C.E.

SYNTHESIS OF FINDINGS

Results of the Literary Analysis

The literary analysis of 2 Baruch has revealed that the book is a carefully composed, intricate document with its own literary integrity. The results of the analysis indicate the incompleteness of previous research on 2 Baruch. R. H. Charles's hypothesis that the book is a collection of sources has been shown to be inadequate. Although the author of 2 Baruch has used a variety of sources and traditions, he has integrated them in a remarkable way to create a literary unity. P.-M. Bogaert has made a valuable contribution to research on 2 Baruch by arguing that the book is a unified composition. His division of the text into symmetrical blocks, however, stops short of explaining how the blocks are related to one another as part of a literary whole. It is this literary integrity of the document as a whole which has been the primary thrust of this dissertation. The composing of this kind of a carefully structured literary work is not unique to 2 Baruch; it is paralleled in other literary works of this time period.[1]

The literary analysis of 2 Baruch has revealed that the primary issues of the book are developed within the unfolding of the story which is being told throughout the document. An approach to the content of 2 Baruch which focuses only on themes is unsatisfactory. Although R. H. Charles, P.-M. Bogaert, and W. Harnisch have isolated and examined various themes within the book, they have left unanswered the question of the relationship of the individual themes to one another and to the whole composition. A sensitivity to the literary structure is necessary in order to understand the nuances of the issues with which the book is concerned.

Finally, the literary analysis of 2 Baruch has shed new light on the relationship between 2 Baruch and 4 Ezra. I have shown that the key to the structure of 2 Baruch is the narrative pattern of grief and consolation identified in 4 Ezra by E. Breech.[2] Moreover, I have argued that, based on this pattern, the text of 2 Baruch reflects much more narrative continuity than does the text of 4 Ezra. In 2 Baruch, the encounters between Baruch and his community are integral to the unfolding of the story. In 4 Ezra, similar encounters between Ezra and his community interrupt the flow of the document and seem to be almost superfluous to the unfolding of the account. The relative lack of narrative continuity in 4 Ezra has not, to my knowledge, been observed previously. It certainly is an important datum in assessing the literary relationship between the two books, and it highlights the literary unity created by the author of 2 Baruch.

2 Baruch as an "Apocalyptic Response"

In recent years, there has been increased research on the phenomenon of apocalyptic thought.[3] This is not the place to discuss in detail the issues involved in this research. Because 2 Baruch is considered to be an

---

[1] For an example of this kind of carefully structured literary work, see N. Peterson, "The Composition of Mark 4:1-8:26," *HTR* 73 (1980) 184-217.

[2] E. Breech, "These Fragments I have Shored against My Ruins: The Form and Function of 4 Ezra," *JBL* 92 (1973) 267-74.

[3] E.g., K. Koch, *The Rediscovery of Apocalyptic* (SBT 2.22; Naperville: Allenson, 1972); J. J. Collins, "Apocalyptic Eschatology as the Transcendence of Death," *CBQ* 36/1 (1974) 21-43; J. J. Collins, "Introduction: Towards the Morphology of a Genre," *Sem* 14 (1979) 1-59.

apocalyptic document,[4] however, it is fitting to conclude this "synthesis of findings" by summarizing the presence and function of apocalyptic motifs in 2 Baruch.

P. Hanson has summarized the characteristics of what he terms "apocalyptic eschatology" and "apocalypticism."[5] His summary provides a helpful overview of this phenomenon. Hanson observes that the social setting for the development of apocalyptic thought is a group experience of alienation. The old structures and institutions lose their viability, and the vacuum therein created threatens life with chaos. There is no one cause for the sense of alienation. It can result from the physical destruction of the structures deemed essential to the community's continued existence. It also can result from tensions within the dominant society, such as those caused by the inroads of Hellenism in the last centuries prior to the common era. Typically, it results in a sharp distinction between the elect and the wicked.

The apocalyptic response to the sense of alienation involves the establishment of a new identity based on the vision of what God is doing on a cosmic level to effect deliverance and salvation. Good and evil frequently assume cosmic dimensions, and sometimes are portrayed as locked in a deadly, dualistic struggle. There often is a deterministic element in this response; history is divided into predetermined periods of time or is perceived as degenerating irrevocably into greater and greater decay. In this setting, salvation is totally removed from the realm of history. God's final act of salvation is perceived as deliverance from the present order to a transformed one, rather than as the fulfillment of His promises within history.

There are both similarities and differences between this description of apocalyptic thought and 2 Baruch. The social setting of 2 Baruch is the experience of group alienation. This alienation is caused both by the physical destruction of Jerusalem and by tensions within the Jewish community. The description of the nature of these tensions—assimilation by Jews to the ways of the Gentiles—is similar to descriptions of "Hellenization" in earlier apocalyptic documents. The typical apocalyptic distinction between the elect and the wicked is refined in 2 Baruch to describe the *few* and the *many*.

The response of 2 Baruch to the sense of alienation involves a vision of God's activities on a cosmic level. The terminology used through-

---

[4]See Koch, *Rediscovery*, 18-22.
[5]P. Hanson, "Apocalypticism," *IDBSup*, 28-34.

out 2 Baruch emphasizes this point; this world is contrasted with the world to come, the present time is contrasted with the eschatological time, and the earth is contrasted with the heavenly realm. Moreover, there is a sense of determinism in 2 Baruch; history is portrayed as a process which is moving toward the inevitable "consummation of times." The connotations of the term "consummation" include a sense of completeness; the end of times will come when the full number of souls, predetermined when Adam sinned, has been born.[6] There is no cosmic dualism between good and evil in 2 Baruch. Although the righteous certainly suffer in this world, this suffering is not attributed to cosmic opponents.

The primary difference between 2 Baruch and the pattern of apocalyptic thought identified by Hanson is the positive assessment of life in this world in 2 Baruch. While it is true that God's power and justice will not be vindicated completely until the eschaton, it is possible to live in this world in firm confidence that God remains loyal to the historical covenants and will guide His people through their historical existence. God's explanation of His chastening activity shows how His justice continues to be effective and active in the present world. The connotations of the word "chasten" imply that present suffering has a positive function. God's explanation of His plan for mankind shows how His power is at work in the historical world. The present is only one part of a vast scenario which extends from the creation to the consummation. Finally, the promise of ongoing leadership for the community illustrates how God will keep His covenantal promises to His people in this world. Thus, while the final resolution of the present situation of alienation still is based on eschatological hope, we see in 2 Baruch an effort also to give hope to the community in its historical existence. By emphasizing the practical question of the reconstruction of the faithful community in the interim time before the consummation, the author of 2 Baruch moves away from apocalyptic speculation and toward the kind of response which will be characteristic of rabbinic Judaism.

In recent research on apocalyptic thought, much emphasis has been placed on the literary aspects of this literature.[7] Sometimes, as in the book of Daniel, the narrative and visionary portions of an apocalyptic

---

[6]Cf. Gal 4:4. Paul uses the term "fullness of time" to refer to the coming of Jesus in the flesh. Here, as in 2 Baruch, the connotations of the term used to describe the consummation include a sense of completion.

[7]See Koch, *Rediscovery*; Collins, "Introduction."

document are neatly distinguished from each other. In 2 Baruch, this is not the case. The whole of 2 Baruch is a narrative; visions and other types of literary genres are integrated into the narrative framework.

IMPLICATIONS AND FURTHER AGENDAS

This dissertation has left unanswered several important questions, which need to be addressed in future research on 2 Baruch. These questions can be summarized briefly.

(1) What was the *Sitz im Leben* of 2 Baruch? We simply do not know the purpose for which the book was composed. P.-M. Bogaert has suggested that parts of 2 Baruch were used as readings in synagogues of the diaspora.[8] This hypothesis, however, is only a conjecture. Bogaert has not shown that 2 Baruch was composed for a diaspora audience.[9] He also has not brought forward sufficient evidence of Jewish liturgical practices in this period. The question of the *Sitz im Leben* of the book remains unanswered.

(2) Is there any relationship between the portrayal of Baruch in 2 Baruch and any known historical figure of the first century C.E.? In a more general sense, can the figure of Baruch as scribe/prophet tell us anything about actual leaders or forms of leadership in this time period? The latter question was raised in Chapter IV.[10] Both questions need to be examined in much greater detail.

(3) What is the relationship of 2 Baruch to rabbinic Judaism?[11] Throughout his book, Bogaert compares themes in 2 Baruch with statements of the rabbis, perhaps implying a closer relationship between 2 Baruch and the rabbinic corpus than the evidence actually indicates. We have seen that 2 Baruch, like the rabbis, is concerned with the practical question of the reconstruction of the community, and that the question of who will interpret the Torah plays an important role in this reconstruction. It is important to examine further how the rabbis interpreted the

---

[8]P.-M. Bogaert, *Apocalypse de Baruch* (SC 144-45; Paris: Le Cerf, 1969) 1. 157-62.

[9]See above, p. 115, n. 28.

[10]See above, pp. 116-17.

[11]This kind of question is raised by J. Strugnell, "Review of Books," *JBL* 89 (1970) 484-85. In a review of Bogaert's book, Strugnell suggests a need to study the whole of apocalyptic Pharisaism of ca. 70 C.E. because it provides one of our very few pieces of direct evidence for rabbinic Judaism in this period.

destructions of 587 B.C.E. and 70 C.E., how they construed the teaching office and prophecy, and whether the identification of "Israel" posed a problem for them in the wake of 70 C.E. It also is important to analyze further their perceptions on suffering and chastisement, and their apocalyptic speculations. Then we may be in a better position to understand the relationship of 2 Baruch to various aspects of rabbinic teaching.

(4) What is the relationship of 2 Baruch to contemporary Christian documents?[12] We have approached this question by comparing 2 Baruch with the Gospel of Matthew. Much more research, however, is needed, particularly in three areas. The Apocalypse of John, like 2 Baruch, refers to the heavenly Temple (chap. 21). In addition, it also reinterprets Daniel 7 in order to describe Rome (e.g., chap. 13). With regard to these and other motifs, the two books need to be examined in order to determine the extent and nature of common traditional materials which are being employed in both documents. The writings of Paul also contain a variety of themes similar to those of 2 Baruch. Like 2 Baruch, Paul raises the question of theodicy in terms of God's faithfulness to His promises, and concludes the discussion with a doxology (Romans 9-11). Like 2 Baruch, Paul talks at length about faith and the relationship of that faith to God's covenant with Abraham (e.g., Romans 1-8). The two sets of writings also contain several similar eschatological motifs (e.g., Galatians 4:4—"the fullness of time"; 1 Corinthians 15:19, 35-54—the discussion on the nature of the resurrection bodies). By comparing the Pauline writings with 2 Baruch from the perspectives of these and other themes, we may gain a better understanding of how common traditions were adapted in different ways as both Jews and Christians struggled to explain how and why God's covenant relationship is effective among His people. Finally, the authors of 2 Baruch and the Gospels utilize a common compositional technique. In both instances, the authors treat the issues with which they are concerned by composing a story in which literary sub-units of various forms and genres are integrated within a narrative framework. The use of this compositional technique provides an interesting point of comparison between these documents.

---

[12]For a list of suggested parallels between 2 Baruch and New Testament writings, see R. H. Charles, *APOT*, 2. 479-80.

Appendix:

An Outline of 2 Baruch

Block 1 (Chapters 1-5)

A.   Narrative Introduction   1:1
B.   Conversation between God and Baruch   1:2-5:4
C.   Narrative Conclusion 5:5-7

Block 2 (Chapters 6-20)

A.   Narrative Introduction and Description   6:1-10:4
B.   Lament by Baruch   10:6-11:7
C.   Discourse by Baruch 12:1-4
D.   Conversation between God and Baruch   chaps. 13-20

Block 3 (Chapters 21-30)

A.   Narrative Introduction   21:1-3
B.   Prayer by Baruch   21:4-25
C.   Conversation between God and Baruch   chaps. 22-30

Block 4 (Chapters 31-43)

A.   Narrative Introduction   31:1-2
B.   Speech by Baruch to the Elders   31:3-32:7
C.   Conversation between Baruch and His Community   32:8-34:1
D.   Lament by Baruch   chap. 35
E.   Vision   chaps. 36-37
F.   Prayer by Baruch   chap. 38
G.   Conversation between God and Baruch   chaps. 39-43

Block 5 (Chapters 44-52)

A. Narrative Introduction   44:1
B. Speech by Baruch to His Successors   44:2-45:2
C. Conversation between Baruch and His Community   chap. 46
D. Narrative   chap. 47
E. Prayer by Baruch   48:2-24
F. Conversation between God and Baruch   48:26-52:7

Block 6 (Chapters 53-76)

A. Narrative Introduction   53:1a
B. Vision   53:1b-11
C. Prayer by Baruch   chap. 54
D. Narrative   55:1-3
E. Conversation between Ramiel and Baruch   55:4-76:4

Block 7 (Chapter 77)

A. Narrative Introduction   77:1
B. Speech by Baruch to His Community   77:2-10
C. Conversation between Baruch and His Community   77:11-17
D. Narrative Conclusion   77:18-26

Bibliography

Ackroyd, P. *Exile and Restoration: A Study of Hebrew Thought of the Sixth Century B.C.* Philadelphia: Westminster Press, 1968.

Atiya, A. S. *A Hand List of the Arabic Manuscripts and Scrolls Microfilmed at the Library of the Monastery of St. Catherine, Mt. Sinai.* Baltimore, 1955.

Bogaert, P.-M. *Apocalypse de Baruch: introduction, traduction du syriaque et commentaire.* SC 144, 45. Paris: Le Cerf, 1969.

Box, G. H., ed. and trans. *The Apocalypse of Abraham.* London: SPCK, 1919.

Breech, E. "These Fragments I have Shored against My Ruins: The Form and Function of 4 Ezra." *JBL* 92 (1973) 267-74.

Cavallin, H. *Life After Death.* ConBNT 7:1. Lund: CWK Gleerup, 1974.

Ceriani, A. M., ed. "Apocalypsis Syriace Baruch." *Monumenta Sacra et Profana.* Vol. 5, Fasc. 4. Mediolani: Bibliotheca Ambrosiana, 1871.

Charles, R. H. *The Apocalypse of Baruch.* London: Black, 1896; repr. London: SPCK, 1917; repr. 1929.

_____. *The Apocrypha and Pseudepigrapha of the Old Testament.* 2 vols. Oxford: Clarendon, 1913; repr. 1963 etc.

Charlesworth, J. *The Pseudepigrapha and Modern Research, with a Supplement.* SCS 7. Chico, CA: Scholars Press, 1981.

Collins, J. "Apocalyptic Eschatology as the Transcendence of Death." *CBQ* 36/1 (1974) 21-43.

_____. "Introduction: Towards the Morphology of a Genre." *Sem* 14 (1979) 1-59.

Collins, M. "The Hidden Vessels in Samaritan Traditions." *JSJ* 3 (1972) 92-115.

Cross, F. M. *The Ancient Library of Qumran and Modern Biblical Studies.* Rev. ed. Garden City: Anchor Books, 1961.

_____. *Canaanite Myth and Hebrew Epic.* Cambridge: Harvard University Press, 1973.

Danby, H., trans. *The Mishnah.* London: Oxford University Press, 1933.

Davies, W. D. *The Gospel and the Land.* Berkeley: University of California Press, 1974.

_____. *The Sermon on the Mount.* Cambridge: Harvard University Press, 1966.

Dedering, S., ed. "Apocalypse of Baruch." *The Old Testament in Syriac.* Part 4, fasc. 3. Leiden: E. J. Brill, 1973.

Denis, A.-M., ed. *Fragmenta pseudepigraphorum quae supersunt graeca.* PVTC 6. Leiden: E. J. Brill, 1970.

Epstein, I., ed. *The Babylonian Talmud.* London: Soncino Press, 1935-1948.

Finkelstein, L., ed. *The Jews: Their History, Culture and Religion.* 2d ed. New York: Harper and Brothers, 1955.

Flusser, D. "The Apocryphal Book of Ascensio Isaiae and the Dead Sea Sect." *IEJ* 3 (1953) 30-47.

Fohrer, G., and Lohse, E. "*Siōn.*" *TDNT* 7 (1971) 300-20.

Frei, H. *Eclipse of Biblical Narrative.* New Haven: Yale University Press, 1974.

Friedländer, M. *Geschichte der jüdischen Apologetik als Vorgeschichte des Christenthums.* Zurich, 1903.

Ginzberg, L. *Legends of the Jews.* Vol. 4. Philadelphia: Jewish Publication Society of America, 1913.

Goldstein, J. "The Apocryphal Book of 1 Baruch." *American Academy for Jewish Research* 46-47 (1979-80) 179-99.

Grant, R. M. *Gnosticism and Early Christianity.* 2d ed. New York: University of Columbia Press, 1966.

Grenfell, B., and Hunt, A., eds. *The Oxyrhynchos Papyri*. London, 1903.

Grundmann, W. "*agathos*." *TDNT* 1 (1964) 10-17.

_____. "*kakos*." *TDNT* 3 (1965) 68-81.

Gry, L. de. "La date de la fin des temps selon les révélations ou les calculs du Pseudo-Philon et de Baruch." *RB* 48 (1939) 345-56.

Hadot, J. "La datation de l'Apocalypse syriaque de Baruch." *Sem* 15 (1965) 79-97.

Hanson, P. "Apocalypse, Genre." *IDBSup* 27-28.

_____. "Apocalypticism." *IDBSup* 28-34.

_____. *The Dawn of Apocalyptic*. Philadelphia: Fortress Press, 1975.

Hare, D. *The Theme of Jewish Persecution of Christians in the Gospel of Matthew*. Cambridge: Harvard University Press, 1967.

Harnisch, W. *Verhängnis und Verheissung der Geschichte: Untersuchungen zum Zeit- und Geschichtsverständnis im 4. Buch Esra und in der syr. Baruchapokalypse*. FRLANT 97. Göttingen: Vandenhoeck & Ruprecht, 1969.

Harrington, D. "Matthean Studies since Joachim Rohde." *HeyJ* 16 (1975) 378-88.

Harrington, D.; Cazeaux, J.; Perrot, C.; Bogaert, P.-M. *Pseudo-Philon: Les Antiquités Bibliques*. SC 229-30. Paris: Le Cerf, 1976.

Hengel, M. *Judaism and Hellenism*. 2 vols. Philadelphia: Fortress Press, 1974.

James, M. R. *The Biblical Antiquities of Philo Now First Translated from the Old Latin Version*. TED. New York: Macmillan, 1971; repr. with prolegomenon by L. H. Feldman, New York: Ktav, 1971.

Jonas, H. *The Gnostic Religion: The Message of the Alien God and the Beginning of Christianity*. Rev. 2d ed. Boston: Beacon Press, 1963.

Jonge, M. de. "Review of Books." *JSJ* 12 (1981) 112-17.

_____. *The Testaments of the Twelve Patriarchs: A Study of Their Text, Composition, and Origin*. 2d ed. Assen: Van Gorcum, 1975.

Josephus. 9 vols. Ed. H. Thackeray, R. Marcus, A. Wikgren, and L. Feldman. Loeb Classical Library. Cambridge: Harvard University Press, 1926-65.

Klausner, J. *The Messianic Idea in Judaism.* New York: Macmillan Co., 1955.

Klein, R. *Israel in Exile.* Philadelphia: Fortress Press, 1979.

Klijn, A. F. J. "Die syrische Baruch-Apokalypse." *Jüdische Schriften aus hellenistisch-römischer Zeit.* 5.2 Gütersloh: Gerd Mohn, 1976.

Kmosko, M., ed. *Liber Apocalypseos Baruch filii Neriae . . . , Epistola Baruch filii Neriae.* Patrologia Syriaca 1:2 Paris: Firmin-Didot et Socii, 1907.

Koch, K. *The Rediscovery of Apocalyptic.* SBT 2.22. Naperville: Allenson, 1972.

Kolenkow, A. C. B. *An Introduction to 2 Baruch 53, 56-74: Structure and Substance.* Harvard Ph.D., 1971.

Koningsveld, P. Sj. "An Arabic Manuscript of the Apocalypse of Baruch." *JSJ* 6 (1975) 205-7.

Köster, H. "*topos.*" *TDNT* 8 (1972) 187-208.

Kraft, R., and Purintun, A.-E., eds. *Paraleipomena Jeremiou.* T and T 1, Pseudepigrapha Series 1. Missoula: SBL, 1972.

Kümmel, G., ed. *Introduction to the New Testament.* 14th rev. ed. New York: Abingdon Press, 1966.

Metzger, B. "Literary Forgeries and Canonical Pseudepigrapha." *JBL* 91 (1972) 3-23.

Montefiore, C., and Loewe, H., eds. *A Rabbinic Anthology.* Cleveland: World Publishing Co.; Philadelphia: Jewish Publication Society of America, 1963.

Moore, G. F. *Judaism in the First Centuries of the Christian Era.* 2 vols. Cambridge: Harvard University Press, 1927-30.

Neusner, J. *Early Rabbinic Judaism.* Leiden: E. J. Brill, 1975.

_____. "Judaism in a Time of Crisis: Four Responses to the Destruction of the Second Temple." *Judaism* 21/3 (1972) 313-27.

_____. *Judaism: The Evidence of the Mishnah.* Chicago: University of Chicago Press, 1981.

New English Bible with the Apocrypha. New York: Oxford University Press, 1961.

Nickelsburg, G. "Enoch, Levi, and Peter: Recipients of Revelation in Upper Galilee." *JBL* 100/4 (1981) 575-600.

_____. "Good and Bad Leaders in the *Biblical Antiquities* of Philo." In *Ideal Figures in Ancient Judaism: Profiles and Paradigms,* pp. 49-65. Ed. J. Collins and G. Nickelsburg. SCS 12. Chico: Scholars Press, 1980.

_____. *Jewish Literature Between the Bible and the Mishnah.* Philadelphia: Fortress Press, 1981.

_____. "Narrative Traditions in the *Paraleipomena of Jeremiah* and 2 Baruch." *CBQ* 35 (1973) 60-68.

_____. *Resurrection, Immortality, and Eternal Life in Intertestamental Literature.* HTS 26. Cambridge: Harvard University Press, 1972.

Nordheim, E. von. *Die Lehre der Alten.* Vol. 1. Leiden: E. J. Brill, 1980.

Peterson, N. "The Composition of Mark 4:1-8:26." *HTR* 73 (1980) 184-217.

Polzin, R. *Moses and the Deuteronomist.* New York: Seabury Press, 1980.

Preisker, H. "*engys.*" *TDNT* 2 (1964) 330-32.

Rad, G. von. *Genesis.* Philadelphia: Westminster Press, 1972.

_____. *The Message of the Prophets.* New York: Harper and Row, 1965.

_____. *Old Testament Theology.* Vol. 2. New York: Harper and Row, 1965.

_____. *Wisdom in Israel.* Nashville: Abingdon Press, 1972.

Roberts, A., and Donaldson, J., trans. *The Ante-Nicene Fathers.* Vol. 1. Grand Rapids: Eerdmans, repr. 1973.

Rohde, J. *Rediscovering the Teachings of the Evangelists.* London: SCM Press, 1968.

Rosenbloom, J. *Conversion to Judaism: From the Biblical Period to the Present.* Cincinnati: Hebrew Union College Press, 1978.

Rosenthal, F. *Vier apokryphische Bücher aus der Zeit und schule R. Akiba's.* Leipzig: O. Schulze, 1885.

Schechter, S. *Aspects of Rabbinic Theology.* New York: Macmillan Co., 1909; repr. Schocken Books, 1961.

Scholem, G. *Major Trends in Jewish Mysticism.* New York: Schocken Books, 1941; Schocken Paperback, 1961; repr. 1974.

Schürer, E. *A History of the Jewish People in the Time of Jesus Christ.* Vol. 3. Edinburgh: T and T Clark, 1897.

Sigwalt, C. "Die Chronologie des syrischen Baruch apokalypse." *BZ* 9 (1911) 397-98.

Smallwood, E. M. *The Jews Under Roman Rule: From Pompey to Diocletian.* Leiden: E. J. Brill, 1976.

Stendahl, K. "Hate, Retaliation, and Love in 1QS x, 10-17 and Romans 12:19-21." *HTR* (1962) 343-55.

Stone, M. "Baruch, Last Words of." *EncJud* 4. 270-71.

_____. *Features of the Eschatology in 4 Ezra.* Harvard Ph.D., 1965.

Strugnell, J. "Review of Books." *JBL* 89 (1970) 484-85.

Suggs, M. J. *Wisdom, Christology, and Law in Matthew's Gospel.* Cambridge: Harvard University Press, 1970.

Thompson, A. L. *Responsibility for Evil in the Theodicy of 4 Ezra.* SBLDS 29. Missoula: Scholars Press, 1977.

Thomson, J. E. H. *Books Which Influenced Our Lord and His Apostles, being a Critical Review of Apocalyptic Literature.* Edinburgh: T and T Clark, 1891.

Tilborg, S. van. *Jewish Leaders in Matthew.* Leiden: E. J. Brill, 1972.

Trilling, W. "Das Wahre Israel." *Studien Zum Alten und Neuen Testament* 10 (1964) 1-244.

Vermes, G. *The Dead Sea Scrolls in English.* 2d ed. New York: Penguin Books, 1975.

Wilder, A. N. *Early Christian Rhetoric.* Cambridge: Harvard University Press, 1971.

Zeitlin, S. "The Apocrypha." *JQR* 37 (1947) 239-48.

Zimmerman, F. "Textual Observations on the Apocalypse of Baruch." *JTS* 40 (1939) 151-56.

Index

HEBREW SCRIPTURES

RABBINIC LITERATURE